INTUITIVE
MANIFESTING

*Align with Your Inner Wisdom
and Attract Your Dream Life*

BRIGIT ESSELMONT

RUNNING PRESS
PHILADELPHIA

Running Press
Hachette Book Group
1290 Avenue of the Americas, New York, NY 10104
www.runningpress.com
@Running_Press

First Edition: October 2024

Published by Running Press, an imprint of Hachette Book Group, Inc.
The Running Press name and logo are trademarks of Hachette Book Group, Inc.

The Hachette Speakers Bureau provides a wide range of authors for speaking events. To find out
more, go to www.hachettespeakersbureau.com or email HachetteSpeakers@hbgusa.com.

Running Press books may be purchased in bulk for business, educational, or promotional use.
For more information, please contact your local bookseller or the Hachette Book Group
Special Markets Department at Special.Markets@hbgusa.com.

The publisher is not responsible for websites (or their content) that
are not owned by the publisher.

Print book cover and interior design by Susan Van Horn

Library of Congress Cataloging-in-Publication Data
Names: Esselmont, Brigit, author.
Title: Intuitive manifesting : align with your inner wisdom and attract your dream life / Brigit Esselmont.
Description: First edition. | Philadelphia : Running Press, 2024. | Includes index.
Identifiers: LCCN 2024027870 (print) | LCCN 2024027871 (ebook) | ISBN 9780762488247 (hardcover) |
ISBN 9780762488254 (ebook)
Subjects: LCSH: Intuition. | Tarot. | Self-actualization (Psychology) | Self-realization.
Classification: LCC BF315.5 .E77 2024 (print) | LCC BF315.5 (ebook) | DDC 153.4/4—dc23/
eng/20240718
LC record available at https://lccn.loc.gov/2024027870
LC ebook record available at https://lccn.loc.gov/2024027871

ISBNs: 978-0-7624-8824-7 (hardcover), 978-0-7624-8825-4 (ebook)

Printed in the United States of America

LSC-C

Printing 1, 2024

CONTENTS

INTRODUCTION: EMBARKING ON A PATH OF INTUITIVE MANIFESTATION

IT WAS A SUNNY SUMMER DAY IN 2012. I WAS SITTING IN a courtyard in Andalucía, Spain, taking in the sights and sounds around me—the chatter of people, the warmth of the sun. My family and I were near the end of our six months traveling the country. As I watched my one- and three-year-old daughters laughing and playing, it hit me that I was at a crossroads. I had a big choice to make about my future. The Universe seemed to pause, waiting to see what I would decide.

I could go back home to Australia and my corporate human resources job, continuing to climb the ranks and pursuing a career path that was feeling more and more uninspiring. Or I could take a leap into the unknown and follow my wild dream of teaching and doing Tarot readings online. It was thrilling—but scary and slightly insane, too.

In that moment, a clarity washed over me that was as broad as the Spanish sky. I saw that my path wasn't fixed. There were infinite possibilities stretching out before me. I was on the brink of cocreation, a point when my deepest desires could become real.

It wasn't just about taking a jump into the unknown, but instead trusting that the Universe could lift me to greater heights than I could imagine. I could feel the electricity of bringing this dream to life, like I was on the edge of something big.

> *The magic in this moment was realizing my power to shape my destiny, to reach beyond limitations into infinite potential. This was the heart of manifestation—not just dreaming, but making dreams real through cocreating with the Universe.*

My intuition told me that this was just the start of something. As I watched my daughters play so joyfully, I knew I had to embrace the dream, lean in to the possibility, and trust in the promise of something more.

On that day in Spain, with the warm sun as my witness, my intuitive manifestation journey began. I set out to turn dreams into reality, aligning with the cosmos to craft a life of meaning and passion. And I made the decision to say a deep, resounding *yes!* to grow my business, Biddy Tarot, and I have never looked back.

That's the wonder of manifestation—a journey sparked by a dream that unfolds into the boundless world of cocreation.

INTUITION IN ACTION: A MOMENT OF CLARITY

Fast-forward to October 2018, six years after I made that pivotal decision to leave behind my corporate career and instead follow my heart and passion with Biddy Tarot. I found myself sitting in a circle of visionary women in South Africa, with Richard Branson across from me. This surreal, yet intensely real, scene was a striking testament to intuition's power.

We spent the day on safari, witnessing the wild savanna's grace and ferocity. At the watering hole, elephants gathered while shielding their young from the painted dogs watching eagerly nearby. Giraffes braved crocodile-infested rivers for a sip of water under the scorching sun. Nearby, a lioness fed on a carcass with her cubs, while a pack of hyenas stalked impalas, eventually taking down and feeding on the weakest among them. Each scene reminded me of life's relentless cycle of trials and triumphs.

As night fell, we gathered around a crackling fire under a sea of stars. The energy of the local tribe's traditional dance came alive through their songs of joy and sorrow, which resonated within each of us. My heart swelled with overwhelming gratitude and connection—to the earth, the people, and the pulsing thread of life.

I felt immense appreciation for the gifts and blessings available to us. Through hardships, challenges, and struggles, there was also beauty, possibility, and abundance. By tapping into life's essence, we find joy and beauty despite difficulties. In that moment, an intuitive clarity washed over me unlike anything I had experienced before. It was as if my inner voice, a subtle lifetime guide, now had a megaphone, reminding me of my power. I had the power to listen deeply, set aligned intentions, take purposeful action, and reach dizzying heights of possibility to manifest my dream life.

Six years after that initial *yes* to Biddy Tarot, I faced another pivotal decision—taking the bold step to expand further and reach millions as a teacher. In this moment, I reaffirmed my trust in intuition. I chose to say *yes* again, but now to an even grander vision—*yes* to aligning with my Higher Self, *yes* to embracing expansion in all facets of life, and *yes* to welcoming abundance openly. This meant saying *yes* to letting intuition guide me on this ambitious path.

No matter the fear, doubt, or resistance I might experience, I was ready to welcome these challenges as catalysts for growth. I committed to honoring and trusting my intuition as my most reliable navigator in expanding my reach and impact. My decision testified to my dedication to evolve, personally and as a leader.

Surrounded by both nature's rawness and human warmth, my path became clear—one paved not just with goals but with an unwavering belief in my intuitive power. This dual understanding exemplified intuitive manifesting—partnering with the Universe in cocreating a reality that resonated with both my mind and soul.

My commitment opened the way to tripling my business revenue, embracing the divine feminine in my practice, and, most importantly, acknowledging my role in the Universe's plan. By aligning with intuition, I could cocreate a reality that harmonized with my soul's desires.

Above all, this turning point taught me to trust—trust the Universe, the journey, and myself.

Reflecting on my intuitive manifestation journey, I see decisive moments woven with intuition's golden thread. It wasn't just about making choices, but also about understanding their origins.

These decisions didn't emerge from logic or a desire for status or wealth. They were born from profound alignment with my Higher Self and Highest Good, guided by intuition's gentle yet unyielding hand.

Integrating intuition transformed my decision-making process. Intuition became my compass through doubts, leading me to outcomes I once only imagined. Each pivotal turn and serendipitous incident appeared not just because I listened, but because I trusted my inner voice implicitly. This trust wasn't blind but part of a process of consciously staying aligned with my true self and values.

That whisper of intuition has been my most faithful advisor. It is the quiet yet powerful force behind the scenes, steering me toward decisions that resonate with my purpose. I have learned to trust that it wasn't sporadic good fortune, but gradual faith in intuition's call, beckoning me toward harmony with the Universe.

This belief shaped Biddy Tarot into what it is today—a thriving ecosystem supporting my family and Team Biddy's fifteen remarkable souls on our mission to share Tarot's power with the world. My inner voice also inspired me to create unforgettable memories—like our six-month family adventures across Spain. These sabbaticals weren't planned on spreadsheets but charted in the heart, led by my soul's longing.

Biddy Tarot started as a small spark—an urge to share my Tarot passion globally. Now it's a beacon of light for millions seeking intuition's guidance through Tarot. Its success shows the power of aligning with your intuition and letting it lead you.

As we explore intuitive manifesting throughout this book, reflect on when intuition has guided your decisions and reshaped your life. What ignited your inner spark? Was it a voice—perhaps one you ignored at first but which grew more insistent? Was there a feeling, a knowing, that something greater called you? These aren't coincidences, but instead your intuitive power's signposts, illuminating your soul's path.

Your story is woven with the same intuitive thread as mine. See yourself not as a passive dreamer, but a bold creator, painting your life with inner wisdom's vibrant colors.

In this book, we'll uncover intuitive manifesting's secrets, igniting your own intuition's spark. You'll learn to listen, recognize the Universe's signs, and craft your reality with intention and clarity. You'll discover the four-step **Intuitive Manifesting Method** that has already helped thousands manifest their dreams.

This is an awakening to your personal power, as you understand your role in reality's fabric and move to your truth's rhythm. It's a transformative process, promising not just fulfillment but a deeper spiritual connection.

By the end, you won't just grasp intuition's power—you'll embody it. Let's chart an extraordinary course guided by your intuition and the Universe as your cocreator. Are you ready to actively shape your unfolding story? Let's begin.

MANIFESTING 101: WHAT IS MANIFESTING?

At the heart of it, manifesting is about bringing your deepest desires to life through focused intention, alignment, and action. It's more than just goal setting; it's a dynamic process of cocreating your life alongside the Universe. It all starts with a personal longing or goal that resonates deeply within you. You shape this longing into a definitive intention. Next comes the crucial part: moving toward your goal in ways that align with it, while staying receptive to the subtle yet transformative nudges the Universe offers. These gentle pushes might redirect you, while always orienting you with your greatest good. Your task? To remain in tune with your intuition and the Universe's wisdom, letting them lead you through this unfolding adventure.

What ignites your passion in manifesting? Is it material abundance, like a shiny new car or a tranquil beach house? Or are you seeking emotional fulfillment—confidence, authenticity, self-love? Maybe you long to nurture deep connections, whether through a soulful partnership or enriching friendships. Manifesting isn't confined by rules; its beauty lies in its diversity and personal touch. Each person's manifesting journey is as unique as their dreams and aspirations.

Here's a glimpse into what members of the Biddy Tarot community[1] are manifesting:

- **Darcie seeks to step into a career as an accomplished writer and intuitive Tarot reader.**

- **Sabina desires a full-body transformation, with daily movement, increased vitality, and healthy, nourishing food.**

- **Kerry is intent on a dreamy, romantic apartment in Paris for her three-month vacation.**

- **Emily sets her sights on growing a thriving business that helps others discover their inner magic.**

- **Kristy pursues a life filled with self-love, overcoming self-doubt to engage positively with the world.**

- **Melanie focuses on becoming debt-free, aligning her finances with her life goals.**

These real-life stories illustrate the diverse potential of manifesting, from tangible objectives like a new home to intangible goals such as self-love. The common thread between them is the essence of manifesting: setting precise intentions, aligning thoughts and actions with these intentions, and entrusting the ride to intuition and the Universe's wisdom.

---

1 Our Biddy Tarot students have generously shared their stories throughout this book to offer inspiration and guidance to you as the reader. Their names have been changed to respect their privacy.

As you journey through this book, you'll learn to wield this potent process, whether you are seeking physical manifestations or profound emotional shifts. You'll discover how to shape your reality with intention and clarity, with intuition as your guiding star.

INTRODUCING INTUITIVE MANIFESTING

Now, let's unveil the heart of this transformative practice—the Intuitive Manifesting Method. This approach integrates a personalized layer to your manifestation work, ensuring your path is not only inspired but also incredibly effective. This approach is unique; it intertwines traditional manifestation methods with a deep connection to our intuitive insights for a more profound impact. Here's a preview of the transformational journey ahead:

INTUITIVE MANIFESTING METHOD

Step One: Picture Your Perfect Future—Sharpen your clarity and set focused intentions that resonate with your Highest Good. Step into this vision with confidence and purpose.

Step Two: Elevate Your Energy Vibration—Tune your energy to match the frequency of abundance. Align your actions with your aspirations, charging them with intention and fire.

Step Three: Break Free from Limiting Beliefs—Uncover and dismantle subconscious barriers. Rewrite the narratives that restrict you and embrace the grand flow of the Universe with trust.

Step Four: Supercharge Your Results—Celebrate every milestone, cultivate gratitude, and master techniques to enhance the effectiveness of your manifestations.

You'll also learn how to become a manifestation magnet as you carry these skills into all facets of your life. But there's more. Throughout this book, you will find an abundance of resources designed not just for learning but for profound *experiential* growth—including meditations, rituals, and Tarot spreads all tailored to boost your manifesting success.

The Intuitive Manifesting Method is comprehensive and empowering. By the book's end, you will have mastered the art of manifesting your desires with joy and ease. Now, as you embrace the potent force of manifestation, get ready to add a transformative element to your practice: the integration of Tarot and intuition. This fusion will upgrade your manifesting from effective to extraordinary, amplifying your capacity to attract and create the life you envision.

MEET YOUR INTUITIVE ALLIES— THE TAROT CARDS

As we've discussed, manifestation isn't just about thought; it's about aligning your energy, your vibration, in harmony with the Universe. To manifest effectively, you need to move beyond limiting beliefs, fears, and doubts, cultivating a wellspring of positivity. Much of this transformative work unfolds in the subconscious, and this is where Tarot shines.

While many people think of Tarot as a mystic, fortune-telling tool exclusive to the gifted few, it is so much more than that. These powerful cards are like the lifeline between you and your intuition, which makes Tarot a faithful manifesting ally.

Tarot is a conduit for intuitive guidance, bridging the mystical realm of intuition and the concrete world of reality. With their evocative imagery and stories, the cards bypass the conscious mind, diving into the subconscious. They illuminate your desires, obstacles, and challenges, bringing them into the light of consciousness. With this newfound clarity, you can interact with them, reshape them, and align your actions with your genuine goals. As you embark on the path of intuitive manifestation, these cards offer profound insights at every step.

Additionally, Tarot aligns you with your Higher Self, fostering the strong lifeline of intuition running between you and ensuring your goals resonate with your highest calling. It's a fantastic tool for tuning in to your inner wisdom. Each card is a channel, magnifying that subtle, inner voice. Their vibrant imagery sparks curiosity and introspection, inviting us to delve into our desires and share these revelations with others.

Throughout this book, we'll explore how Tarot and intuition can intertwine to elevate your manifestation efforts. With each chapter, you'll dive into Tarot wisdom, enriching your understanding of yourself and illuminating your manifestation journey. You'll be introduced to archetypes, spreads, techniques, and thought-provoking questions that deepen your connection to this powerful practice.

Let's start with the Fool, which represents the beginning of our Tarot journey. Like the first page of a new journal, the Fool symbolizes the raw potential that awaits us. It invites us to step into the unknown with an open heart and an eagerness to explore. As we embark on this journey in which intuition becomes our guiding light, the Fool reminds us of the endless possibilities that await when we trust in the power of our inner wisdom.

THE FOOL: THE JOURNEY BEGINS

The Fool is the embodiment of new beginnings and akin to standing on the precipice of a cliff with the unknown calling out to you. This card symbolizes the heart-led leap into new experiences, driven more by instinct than by the meticulous calculations of the mind. It embodies the excitement that surges within us as we embark on uncharted paths.

In the realm of intuitive manifesting, the Fool is our symbol of unwavering trust in the Universe's grand design. It represents

THE FOOL

the exhilaration of potential, the state in which we are unhindered by preconceived limits. It's about embracing fear and proceeding regardless. This leap is not about heedless risk-taking; rather, it's a testament to the courage that allows us to understand that the journey's value is as significant as that of the destination.

The Fool encourages us to take that first step, even when every detail isn't precisely laid out—especially then. It invites us to break free from the paralysis of overthinking or the need to control every outcome. This card teaches us to shed doubts and trust the inner wisdom that whispers, *Now is your time.*

The Fool doesn't merely walk—he dances on the edge of tomorrow, unburdened by the weight of worry and doubt. This card challenges us to realize that the perfect moment we often wait for is already upon us.

Manifesting with the Fool's Spirit

View your current phase as filled with potential. When the Fool is in play, the world is indeed your oyster. This is your cosmic signal to embrace spontaneity and let your creativity roam free in the landscape of possibilities. Guided by the Fool, approach your ideas with the assurance of someone who believes in the wonder of new beginnings.

The Fool reminds us that life is both a journey and a playground. It's an invitation to loosen up, to revel in laughter, and to sync your steps with life's vibrant rhythm. This card urges you to see the world with wonder and let your heart lead with uninhibited joy.

The Fool as Meditation for Overcoming Fear

When fear or self-doubt looms, call upon the spirit of the Fool for clarity. This intrepid traveler isn't just a Tarot figure; he reflects the purest aspects of you—your wild spirit, your carefree inner child, and your joyous soul. He doesn't dismiss fear; he recognizes it and strides forward in spite of it.

So seize the opportunity. Allow the Fool to guide you beyond your comfort zone into the realm of potential and possibility. Ask yourself, *What have I got to lose by saying yes to this opportunity? What have I got to gain?*

INTUITIVE MANIFESTATION IN PRACTICE: THE FOOL'S LEAP

Reflection

In your journal or a notebook, reflect on the following questions and write down your insights . . .

- **What has been your manifesting journey throughout your life? What have you manifested? How? What has worked for you? And what hasn't?**

- **What would manifesting look like for you if you were to awaken to the call of your own intuition? What would be possible?**

Ritual

As you begin this journey of intuitive manifesting, embrace the energy of the Fool. Imagine yourself at the edge of a cliff—will you take the leap into the unknown? Or will you step back to safety, never knowing what might have happened if you had said yes to opportunity. And what happens when you do take that giant leap off the cliff? Do you fall or do you fly? What becomes possible for you?

Imagine this in your mind's eye, and as you do, just observe the feelings, the emotions, the thoughts, and the self-talk that may arise. There's no need to judge and analyze. Instead, take the opportunity to notice what comes up when you embrace the energy of the Fool.

What resistance do you need to let go of? What new opportunities can you embrace? This is all part of saying *yes* to this exciting journey into the unknown and trusting your intuition.

THE THRESHOLD OF INTUITION AND MANIFESTATION

Our foundational understanding is now set, and we're ready to cocreate with the Universe as we turn intuition into manifestation. As we stand on this threshold with the Fool as our ally, we're ready to move forward. In the chapters that follow, you'll discover the pillars of intuitive manifestation, each building on the last, guiding you toward a life lived in deep alignment with your truest self. Now, let's take that first step together, turning intuition into powerful action in chapter one.

· ○ ○ ✳ ○ ○ ·

PART I: FOUNDATIONS OF INTUITIVE MANIFESTING

Your intuition has guided you here, to a place where your heart's truths align with the Universe's possibilities. This is our starting point—the sacred space within ourselves where dreams and universal energies intertwine.

In the coming chapters, we'll explore the essential principles of intuitive manifesting. Imagine manifesting as a river, effortlessly flowing and navigating around obstacles with grace. Like water, your aspirations find their way, guided by faith and trust. Here, your soul's deepest desires blend with the generous flow of universal energy.

Part one is about recognizing your potential as a powerful creator. The Universe is not just a backdrop to your desires but an active participant, eager to collaborate with your vision. Learn to trust the whispers that suggest a pause, the nudges that propel you forward, and the serendipitous signs that untrained eyes often miss.

Throughout this section, we'll nurture your inner landscape, preparing it for the dreams you wish to seed and cultivate. Each insight will enrich your spirit, setting the stage for growth and flourishing. Before taking action, we'll focus on being—tuning in to the Universe's rhythms and your intuition's subtle language.

By the end of part one, you'll have established a deep connection with your inner wisdom and a harmonious partnership with the Universe. You'll be ready, with a heart full of dreams and hands open to receive, to embrace the art of intuitive manifesting as a gracious recipient and honored cocreator.

CHAPTER ONE:

Cocreating with the Universe

THERE COMES A MOMENT WHEN COCREATION WITH THE
Universe transforms from an abstract concept into vibrant reali-
ty—a moment electrified by realizing you're not alone on this grand
journey. For me, this awakening occurred in 2016, nestled with my
family of four in a Melbourne town house.

While our neighborhood was buzzing with lively restaurants,
cafés, and shops and we were surrounded by friends, we still felt
a deep longing for something more—something that the city's

suburbs couldn't provide. We yearned for nature, sunshine, and a richer, more authentic sense of life.

This deep-seated yearning was our unconscious initiation into the process of cocreation. Without fully realizing it, by acknowledging our desire for change, we were sending a powerful signal to the Universe—an invitation to begin a collaborative journey toward our true aspirations.

During a family holiday up north, where the sun's rays felt warmer and the beaches stretched endlessly, we explored three different locales. Two didn't resonate with us, but the Sunshine Coast captured our hearts instantly. Buoyed by this newfound love, we scoured the area for a house, but our search seemed in vain. We returned to Melbourne, a 2.5-hour flight back, carrying a seed of hope that somehow the perfect home would find us. Something within me told me that it would happen and faster than we would realize.

Emboldened by this hope, we arranged another trip, leaving our kids with their grandparents. In a whirlwind thirty-six hours, we toured nine houses. Each had potential—all hovering at an eight out of ten—but none were "the one." I felt tempted to settle for "almost right," yet a voice within urged me not to compromise. And while I didn't know it at the time, this reluctance to settle was essential. That feeling was about aligning our actions with our heart's deepest longings, refusing to settle for anything less than what truly resonated.

In our last hours on the Sunshine Coast over coffee in a local café, we revisited our options feeling a mix of hope and weariness. That's when my husband brought up a house he had kept an eye on—a dream home priced beyond our budget but with an open house happening in just an hour. His suggestion sparked a twinkle in my eye. "Are we ready to fall in love with a home we might not be able to afford?" I asked. His reply was resolute: "Yes, let's do it!"

As we drove down the driveway lined with stunning jacarandas in full bloom, my heart fluttered with excitement. The house was a haven, embraced by five acres of nature, rainforest, and tropical plants. Every room had floor-to-ceiling windows bringing the outside world in and blurring the lines between nature and our living space. But it was the sight of Tarot cards in the final room that sealed it for me—a clear sign from the Universe. This was our home.

We returned to Melbourne with our hearts ablaze. But the challenge was real, and our minds wrestled with the practicalities. Our Melbourne home needed to sell for far more than estimated to make this dream viable. It seemed like a long shot, but we trusted in the Universe and went forward. On auction day for our town house, we huddled on our staircase listening as the bids outside climbed—one after another, soaring beyond our reserve and reaching the crucial amount we needed. And then, it happened—the gavel fell, and our dream was a reality. We had dared to trust, and the Universe had not just responded: it had embraced our dreams as well.

This journey transcended finding a home. It profoundly revealed the power of cocreation, of entrusting ourselves to the Universe's grand design. Against the odds, it showed me how aligning our deepest desires with the Universe's rhythm manifests magic.

This partnership, this mystical alliance, balances
intention and intuition, action and surrender,
dreaming and doing.

THE UNIVERSE IS YOUR CREATIVE PARTNER

Cocreation, as I've come to understand it, is an intentional partnership between your deepest desires and the universal energy that interconnects us all. It's about initiating action with the conviction that the Universe is not just a passive observer, but an active participant in bringing your dreams to life. You are working with the Universe, and the Universe is working with you.

This chapter dives into the heart of cocreation, guiding you to unlock your manifesting potential and draw your visions into reality, in harmony with the Universe's energies.

Let's be real, though, because we can stumble on the journey of manifesting when we lose this sacred alignment. Some sit back, casting their dreams skyward like wishes into the wind, passively awaiting the Universe's intervention. Others forge ahead with unyielding determination, driven by ego, attempting to mold the world with brute force. Both approaches miss the delicate balance that is the essence of cocreation.

Imagine this: You feel a calling to change where you live and, inspired by what you see on Instagram or in magazines, you decide that living by the beach in a beautiful home is what you truly desire.

Driven by this dream, you might start by taking focused action to find your ideal beachfront property. But while you're busy doing all the things to make your dream home come true, the Universe has other ideas, and you experience obstacle after obstacle. You keep pushing and pushing, trying to make it happen, but the Universe is shouting, "No! This isn't for you!"

Alternatively, you might just leave everything up to the Universe. You create a vision board with stunning seaside images—but you're imagining the salt air and sandy toes without taking any concrete steps. In this passive state, you're simply adrift, waiting for the dream to materialize on its own.

But what if you truly embraced cocreation? What if you start by reflecting on what you genuinely seek in a home. Perhaps you realize it's not merely a beach house you desire, but a space that nourishes your soul and connects you with nature. A vision of a home in the hinterland emerges, not just as a living space but as the inspiration for a lifestyle—with lush gardens, a patch for vegetables, and the tranquility of nature. With this redefined vision, you begin to align your actions with your intentions, exploring new locations and considering possibilities you hadn't thought of before.

And then, the perfect hinterland home appears, not just as a dwelling, but as a sanctuary. Here, you can tend to your garden, bask in nature's serenity, and welcome friends and family into a generous, warm space. What once seemed like a compromise becomes a revelation. This home, with its deep connection to nature and room for growth, surpasses the initial charm of a beachfront property. The ephemeral allure of the beach pales in comparison to the enduring, vibrant life offered by your hinterland retreat.

By embracing cocreation, you realize that the Universe sometimes guides you not toward the dream you initially envisioned but toward a reality that is far more enriching and in tune with your true self.

Cocreation isn't about dictating terms to the Universe or resigning yourself to fate. It's about acknowledging the Universe as a collaborative partner in manifesting your dreams.

In cocreating with the Universe, you begin to attune to the subtle synchronicities that mark your path—the recurring symbols, patterns, and pieces of advice that gently guide your way. You understand and move in harmony with the Universal Laws of Manifesting, aligning not through resistance but in a rhythm of graceful acceptance and surrender to the forces shaping our existence.

Here, the power of intuitive tools, particularly Tarot, becomes instrumental. They act as conduits, helping you tune in to these signs. Tarot reading serves as a mirror, reflecting deeper insights back to you and highlighting the subtle cues the Universe sends your way. By consulting Tarot, you engage in a dialogue with the Universe, gaining clarity and confirmation on your journey, ensuring your steps are in sync with the natural, guiding flow of life.

THE UNIVERSAL LAWS OF MANIFESTING

Understanding the Universal Laws of Manifesting becomes crucial as we journey deeper into cocreation with the Universe. These laws are as real and unyielding as the physical laws governing our world. They are the unseen yet powerful forces that shape energy, consciousness, and the materialization of our deepest dreams. By grasping these laws, we can sculpt our lives in partnership with the Universe. Let's explore each one in more depth.

The Law of Attraction

The Law of Attraction goes beyond mere positive thinking. It acknowledges the potent force of our focused thoughts and unwavering beliefs in shaping our external reality. By channeling our mental energy toward desired outcomes, we attract aligned experiences, drawing them to us with the inevitability of gravity. Conversely, fixating on negative thoughts can unwittingly invite unwanted experiences into our lives. Consider one of my students, Alise, who dreamed of a fulfilling career as an intuitive healer. Every day, she visualized herself as a clear channel for insight, helping dozens of clients release their limitations and live to their highest potential, as she felt the deep fulfillment and satisfaction of her role. As a result, her steadfast focus and belief gradually brought her vision into reality, presenting opportunities that matched her aspirations.

The Law of Vibration

The Law of Vibration teaches us that every part of the cosmos, including ourselves, resonates with its own energy. When we attune our personal energy to resonate with that of our goals, the Universe reciprocates, crafting realities in line with our intentions. By aspiring toward our Highest Good, we invite an elevated state of being and experience that often surpasses our expectations. I think of this as "being then doing," a powerful idea we'll explore further in this book (see page 87). *Be* and then *do*; align with your Highest Good, and doors open to a world of possibilities.

For instance, if you're seeking a harmonious relationship, embodying love and understanding in your own being attracts similar energy in a partner. You will be seeking love not just by wanting it, but by being a vessel of love and compassion, thereby attracting similar energy.

The Law of Action

The Law of Action emphasizes the importance of active participation in realizing our dreams. Visualization lays the groundwork, but purposeful action brings aspirations to fruition. John dreamed of being an artist. While he visualized his success, he also took proactive steps like going to classes and networking to bridge the gap between his desires and their actualization.

The Law of Gratitude

Gratitude acts as a magnet for prosperity. With the Law of Gratitude, we learn that thankfulness is not passive; it's an active state of appreciation that, when practiced, multiplies the good in our lives. By actively practicing gratitude, we align with the frequency of abundance, setting the stage for more joy and growth. When Emily expressed genuine gratitude for her small business's success, she not only enjoyed her achievements, but also opened doors to new opportunities and expansion.

The Law of Detachment

The Law of Detachment teaches the art of release and the acceptance of the fluid nature of the Universe. It teaches us to loosen our white-knuckled grip on specific expectations and trust in the ebb and flow of opportunity and possibility. When we detach, we don't disengage from our goals; instead, we open ourselves to the full spectrum of potential outcomes, welcoming experiences that may far outshine our initial aspirations. By freeing ourselves from fixed outcomes, we open up to a spectrum of possibilities, allowing for unexpected and often more fulfilling results.

— ⊄◯◯⊅ —

These laws work in concert with one another, each playing a vital role in manifestation. When your thoughts align with positive intentions (Attraction), your energy resonates with these intentions (Vibration), you take proactive steps (Action), revel in gratitude (Gratitude), and stay open to varied outcomes (Detachment), a powerful synergy emerges. This synergy lifts your desires from mere dreams to tangible realities.

Take a moment to reflect on instances in your life where these laws subtly steered your course. Maybe a serendipitous encounter that led to a significant opportunity was the Universe responding to your vibrational state. Or an apparent setback that guided you to a more suitable path was the Law of Detachment in action. Acknowledging these laws at work in your life enhances your connection with the Universe's abundance, enabling you to navigate your journey with deeper awareness and purpose.

As you progress through this book, you'll see these laws intricately woven into its fabric. By the end, you'll be adept at using them intuitively to manifest your dreams into reality. In fact, take a moment now to reflect on how they have already played a role in your life, paving the way for a profound bond with the Universe's endless abundance.

CONNECTING WITH THE UNIVERSE'S ABUNDANCE

You are here to live in true abundance—with a richness within and surrounding you, graciously offered by universal love. Embracing cocreation means accepting this infinite abundance as your inherent right. This act sets up a contract between you and the Universe and the promise of unlimited support in achieving your Highest Good. Your role is simply to say *yes* wholeheartedly to these gifts, receiving them with an open heart and mind. When you do, opportunities and manifestations flow easily. However, fear, resistance, doubt, or control can inadvertently block the bounty intended for you.

Abundance isn't about having more. It's about recognizing the Universe as an endless source of energy and opportunity. Moving from an orientation of scarcity to a mindset rich with possibilities unlocks a reality in which abundance is palpable and dynamic.

This perspective transforms our understanding of success. In the Universe's design, your success amplifies prosperity for all. As you reach your goals, you become a beacon, igniting and fostering success in others. This is the essence of manifesting—believing in collective, thriving potential. It dissolves guilt around ambitious aspirations. Your rise becomes a guiding light, illuminating paths for many.

Consider Jenny's experience with intuitive manifesting: "I believed desiring more was greedy, so I never asked the Universe for anything extra. Even the things I did have, like my vacation home, I kept quiet about, feeling it was boasting [to share about them]. Now I understand I must express gratitude for what I have and also desire more—bigger goals, opportunities, travel, joy, family time, and abundance. Learning that the Universe encourages my expansion has been a revelation."

This approach dismisses the myth of a zero-sum game, where everyone is in competition for a limited supply of good things, instead revealing ever-expanding potential through which each person's triumph contributes to collective prosperity in a Universe of unlimited abundance. Challenging the notion that one person's success diminishes another's unlocks boundless opportunities for all. Each realized dream celebrates the Universe's limitless generosity—a bounty we all share.

Once you embrace this mindset of abundance, the next step is attuning yourself to the Universe's guidance. Attuning begins with *listening*. Amid life's hustle, we often get caught in constant *doing* rather than simply *being*—being present in nature, attuned inwardly, immersed in the world's wonders. In stillness, we hear the Universe's subtle guidance—synchronistic opportunities, nature's messages, and intuitive nudges.

This connection takes practice. As you cultivate stillness, you'll begin to hear the Universe's whispers. Once you are attuned, communication becomes powerful. Ask meaningful questions, and the Universe responds through visions, words, sensations, or intuitive knowing. Practices like journaling, meditating, and Tarot reading open a clear channel between you and the Universe, facilitating easier communication.

This transcends just contemplating goals and desires. You work alongside the Universe, moving beyond ego to manifest your dreams. Attuning yourself also reveals your true capabilities.

We often underestimate our potential when we are constrained by self-imposed limits and doubts. Tapping into the Universe's infinite potential reveals our capacity for far greater achievements. Consider your growth over the past few years. What once seemed unattainable to you is now visible progress that you've made. Looking ahead, allow yourself to expand your mindset, embracing limitless potential. Let intuition unveil possibilities beyond imagination—the Universe can help you step beyond limitations into your true capabilities.

With this expanded perspective, you can then focus on aligning with your Highest Good. Aligning is like flowing with a river—your actions become purposeful and your path unfolds gracefully. This alignment sets intentions that resonate with higher purpose, maintaining flow that naturally draws you toward your true calling.

When you are aligned with the Highest Good for all, your journey seamlessly flows with life. This mindset acknowledges that your fulfillment interconnects with others' well-being. Aspiring for the Highest Good creates a reality imbued with positivity and purpose.

For example, Becky initially aimed to welcome three new friends in six months. However, she realized her true desire wasn't just about expanding her social circle. It was about how she wanted to be in the world—radiating an open heart, sharing love and compassion in every interaction. This shift brought a beautiful transformation. Not only did Becky's circle of friends grow, but she also became deeply involved in her community, living her intention through volunteer work and leading a monthly crafting circle. By embracing love and compassion, she touched more lives than she could have imagined, far surpassing her original goal.

In every aspiration, there is an opportunity to serve ourselves and others. Pursuing our goals can simultaneously contribute positively to those around us. Whether by sharing positive energy or actively assisting others, this approach amplifies impact, making achieving our aspirations a collective success.

All this requires staying connected to your intuition. Intuition acts as a bridge between you and abundance, voices your desires, and keeps you aligned to serve your Highest Good and others' as well. Without it, the journey loses meaning. But with intuition, every step is purposeful and guided, as it taps into your boundless potential.

THE EMPRESS: CREATIVITY AS A CATALYST

In the Tarot world, there lies a figure of lush promise and profound creative power—the Empress. She emerges as our guide, taking us from the celestial embrace of universal alignment to the fertile fields of personal empowerment. The Empress is a wellspring of creative and nurturing energy, which is essential for manifestation. She embodies the very essence of life's generosity and abundance.

16

As the universal symbol of fertility and boundless creative expression, the Empress plays a crucial role in our intuitive manifestation journey. She represents our desires in their most tangible form and envelops them with the nurturing care they need to manifest into our reality.

Imagine the Empress enthroned amid flourishing fields and meandering rivers in her glorious domain. Her presence epitomizes growth, prosperity, and nature's nurturing embrace. More than just a symbol of creation, the Empress represents the continuous caretaking that is essential for the thriving of all endeavors, be they personal projects or expansive visions. She encourages us to plant our intentions deliberately and tend to them with love and patience, honoring the natural rhythm of growth and development.

The Empress's harmony with her environment is a lesson in interconnectedness. She thrives in unison with her surroundings, both nurturing and being nurtured by the world around her. This symbiosis invites us to cultivate a similar balance in our own lives—whether in our homes, workplaces, or relationships. We mirror the Empress's harmony with her world by intentionally creating spaces where our intentions can root and flourish.

Embracing the Empress's Energy

How, then, do we enfold the Empress's essence into our lives? It begins in the mind, by opening ourselves to the nurturing abundance surrounding us and cultivating a receptive mindset. This mindset extends into our lifestyle choices as we embrace and cherish the natural world, drawing upon Earth's grounding energies.

Our spiritual practices become conduits for connecting with the Empress's fertile spirit. Engaging in rituals and meditations aligns us with her loving and abundant energy, strengthening our bond with the creative forces of the Universe.

As much as we commit to manifesting our desires, we must remain open to the Universe's gifts. By welcoming the flow of abundance that nurtures and enriches our creations, we allow our aspirations to blossom fully. In doing so, we embody the Empress's spirit—fostering growth, embracing abundance, and living in harmony with the nurturing forces of the Universe.

INTUITIVE MANIFESTATION IN PRACTICE: THE EMPRESS'S RITUALS AND REFLECTIONS

Nature's Offering

Here's an intuitive ritual that can help you connect with the energy of abundance, beauty, and gratitude. Venture into the natural world and gather elements that speak to your soul—be it flowers, leaves, feathers, stones, or twigs. As you gather, connect with the spirit of each element. If you're picking from a living plant, ask for permission with respect, ensuring you leave plenty behind.

Create a mandala on the earth, using these natural treasures. With each placement, weave in your gratitude and appreciation for the endless beauty and abundance surrounding you. Let this mandala be a sacred expression of your connection to Mother

Earth. When your mandala is complete, offer a heartfelt prayer or blessing, dedicating this creation to Mother Earth as a token of your gratitude to the nurturing forces of nature.

Abundance Tarot Reading

Do this reading when you wish to deepen your connection with the essence of abundance. Before you begin, hold your Tarot deck and close your eyes. Tune in to the energy of abundance—sense what abundance feels like, hear what abundance sounds like, see what abundance looks like. Let this energy permeate every cell of your being.

When you feel ready, gently open your eyes, and pull a card for each of these reflective questions:

1. **How is abundance currently manifesting in my life?**

2. **In what ways might abundance unfold in my future?**

3. **What steps can I take to attract more abundance?**

4. **How can I open myself to receive greater abundance?**

5. **What are the ways I can express my gratitude for abundance?**

Trust your intuition as you interpret each card. If you feel called to do so, explore the meanings at www.biddytarot.com. Journal your thoughts, letting your intuition flow freely. Conclude your reading by giving thanks for the abundance in your life and the prosperity yet to come, acknowledging the Universe's role in this endless cycle of giving and receiving.

UNLOCKING YOUR LIMITLESS POTENTIAL

In true cocreation, the journey unfolds with almost ethereal ease, as if it were predestined. You'll find yourself surpassing the realms of ordinary logic, tapping into a reservoir of potential that may seem elusive to your conscious mind, yet is deeply understood by the Universe.

Embracing cocreation opens you to a world where magic is real and outcomes extend beyond mere personal desires, reaching for the collective Highest Good. It's about adopting the kind of trust eloquently described by Gabrielle Bernstein—the profound belief that the Universe indeed has your back.

However, it's important not to mistake cocreation for mere wish-making. It's a shared endeavor; you and the Universe both play your parts. Your active engagement is crucial. Without it, you might find yourself caught up in an ego-driven uphill battle, where achievements might feel unfulfilling, lacking true resonance with your deepest self and the Universe's grand design.

Ultimately, cocreation resides in the sweet spot between intention and surrender, between making things happen and letting them happen. It's about actively shaping your path and allowing the Universe to weave its magic into the pattern. This delicate equilibrium is the secret to transforming existence into an extraordinary adventure, marked by deep alignment with the universal flow.

∘ ○ ✳ ○ ∘ •

CHAPTER TWO:

A Holistic Approach to Manifesting

ARE YOU READY TO EXPLORE INTUITIVE MANIFESTATION? This journey goes far beyond merely ticking boxes on a wish list; it's about creating a sacred alignment as we weave our deepest desires with the core of our true selves. Here, we intertwine our actions, subconscious beliefs, and spiritual energies, synchronizing them with our genuine intentions. This process is not just a means to an end, but rather a transformative crucible, an alchemical reaction that reshapes our external circumstances and ignites profound shifts within ourselves.

In today's fast-paced world, manifesting is often depicted through glossy images of luxury and success: dream homes, exotic holidays, and tales of overnight fortunes. This mainstream interpretation of manifesting, adorned with glamour and promises of swift success, has become ubiquitous, from the pages of self-help books to the ever-present social media landscape. But let's be real for a moment: this glittering portrayal may not always hold the key to true fulfillment—and it doesn't always work.

The traditional view of the manifestation process is often framed as a straightforward, almost magical formula: set your intention, believe fervently, and *voilà*—you'll receive. It champions positive thinking, vivid visualization, and the certainty of materializing one's desires. This approach encourages aiming for the stars and pursuing extravagant dreams.

While these techniques can be effective and catalyze change, they capture only part of the picture. Traditional methods of manifesting can oversimplify, suggesting that thoughts alone can draw your desires into reality. Moreover, they often neglect the vital aspect of aligning your aspirations with your Highest Good and choosing goals that truly resonate on a deeper, more internal level beyond societal expectations or external validation.

And yet manifesting has undeniably resonated with so many— and its popularity has somewhat diluted the practice's core message. Despite its widespread appeal, mainstream manifesting's focus on quick, material gains often overshadows its deeper, more transformative aspects. This superficial approach risks disillusionment when instant results don't materialize or when achieved goals fail to deliver the anticipated satisfaction. Is it any wonder, then, that this focus on quick external fixes often yields less-than-stellar results—if it brings any results at all?

True manifesting—*intuitive* manifesting—involves both internal transformation and reaching external objectives, inviting intro-spection, personal growth, and deeper self-connection. This path may not be as glamorous or yield immediate results, but it prom-ises a more meaningful and enduring fulfillment.

So let's move beyond the surface allure of mainstream meth-ods. Let's embrace a more holistic approach that values the jour-ney as much as the destination and nurtures our deepest selves along with our worldly ambitions. This is the path to genuine, last-ing transformation—a journey not just to what we want but to who we truly are.

A HOLISTIC PATH TO LASTING TRANSFORMATION

Let's talk about Melanie, a student from my Intuitive Manifesting program. Before starting the course, Melanie, like many of us, tried to shake off her financial struggles. Armed with a vision board full of dollar signs and abundant hope, she set out to manifest finan-cial freedom. Day in, day out, she visualized and affirmed, all while practicing gratitude. But, after a whole month of this intense effort, she was back to square one—nothing had changed.

It's a familiar story, right? Melanie's intention was clear, but something crucial was missing. Her journey to wealth wasn't really meshing with who she was deep down. She was playing the manifesting game, but it wasn't rooted in her true self. And her intuition? Well, it was pretty much left out of the conversation.

Then Melanie discovered my Intuitive Manifesting Method, and that's when she had a massive aha moment. She realized manifesting isn't just about visualizing an outcome; it's about harmonizing that vision with your authentic self. Intuition is not just an accessory; it's the cornerstone of the manifesting process. Intuition creates a bridge between our deepest desires and our true purpose, guiding us toward actions that resonate with our inner wisdom.

This new approach was transformative for Melanie. She began to tune in, really listening to her inner voice and letting it steer her choices and actions. This wasn't just about getting rich anymore. It was about aligning her financial aspirations with her true self, guided by intuition and the principles of intuitive manifesting. This shift not only brought her closer to financial freedom, but also empowered her personal growth. Within months, her life began to feel more abundant than ever before, and she enjoyed this new level of freedom.

If your manifesting attempts feel a little tired or superficial, consider these key truths:

Your intentions must be crystal clear. Without a clear understanding of your true desires, manifesting is aimless. Direct your energy toward goals that genuinely resonate with you.

Alignment is everything. If your aspirations aren't in harmony with your inner truth, they may manifest with unintended consequences or not manifest at all, as they lack heart and genuine intention.

Actions speak louder. Mere wishing is insufficient. Manifesting requires actions that resonate with your aspirations.

Your mindset is a magnet. Align your thoughts and energy with your goals. A mismatched mindset can repel what you wish to attract.

Blocks are real. Everyone has mental blocks. Recognize and work through them, or they'll stop your manifesting in its tracks.

Manifestation *is not* an instant-gratification game. Manifesting isn't instantaneous; it demands consistency, trust, and patience.

Manifestation *is* a holistic, life-changing practice. It's more than achieving desires; it's a lifestyle, a path of empowerment, a belief in your worthiness to receive and create.

Intuition is key. Intuition is not a nice-to-have; it's the guiding force of your manifesting journey, aligning you with your Highest Good.

Traditional manifesting often overlooks these essentials, focusing more on material outcomes than the inner journey.

Intuitive manifesting is a whole different ball game. It's not just about the things you want to attract. It's about aligning those desires with the deepest parts of yourself, balancing your actions, subconscious beliefs, and energies—all in tune with your true intentions. Here lies the real magic, through which you transform both your external and internal worlds.

So how do you get your actions to line up with your deeper intentions? The key is to tune in to your intuition, that inner voice that whispers truths we sometimes ignore or drown out in the course of our busy lives. Whether we tap into this voice through meditation, nature walks, journaling, or Tarot, the goal is to open a clear channel for your intuition to flow and guide your path.

Intuitive manifesting invites the Universe into your journey. It's about aligning your heart, soul, and mind with your goals, creating a vibrational match that draws your desires closer. When what's inside you matches what you're aiming for, the Universe listens and responds.

So consider this an invitation to evolve your manifesting approach. Move beyond the standard playbook and step into a realm where intuition leads and the Universe collaborates with you. And engage your whole self—mind, body, and spirit—and recognize each part's role in turning dreams into reality.

In the sections to come, we'll explore the elements of manifestation and how blending them with intuition creates a powerful concoction that brings our deepest desires to life.

ELEMENTS OF MANIFESTATION: INTENTION, ALIGNMENT, AND ACTION

As we dive deeper into the idea of holistic manifesting, we find three key players: intention, alignment, and action. Each one has a crucial role in turning our dreams from wisps of imagination into concrete reality.

Intention is where it all starts, the very seed from which our dreams grow. But what exactly is intention? It's more than just a wish or a hope; it's a crystal clear, focused declaration and a conscious message to the Universe announcing, "This is my heart's true desire."

The psychology behind setting intentions is fascinating. Intentions sharpen our focus and direct our energies toward a specific aim. They guide our thoughts, emotions, and actions, aligning us with our goals. The more precise and specific the intention, the stronger and clearer the message we convey to the Universe.

Next comes **alignment**. This is all about making sure our intentions resonate harmoniously with our authentic selves and the universal flow. Here, intuition takes center stage. Alignment is about feeling a deep-rooted affirmation that says, "Yes, this path is genuinely meant for me."

When our goals don't align with our true nature or the greater good, they can seem forced or hollow. Achieving such misaligned goals might leave us feeling empty or disconnected. However, true alignment brings ease, flow, and a sense of correctness, signaling that we're traveling the right path.

Finally, we arrive at **action**—the tangible steps we take to bring our intentions to fruition. But we're not talking about just any actions; we're referring to inspired actions. These are actions born from a place of alignment and intention. They are infused with energy and meaning, and taking them feels as though we're seamlessly moving with the current of life.

Inspired action is about attuning to our intuition, heeding that inner wisdom, and then making moves that feel perfectly in sync with our objectives. It's as if the Universe itself is giving us a gentle push, whispering, "This is your moment. Go for it!"

By blending intention, alignment, and action, we create a powerful concoction. It's a magical formula that shifts our dreams from the realm of thought into tangible reality. And it's what makes intuitive manifesting so different from the more traditional models of manifesting.

Now that we've got the basics, let's take it up a level and move into a more mystical and often overlooked aspect of manifesting: the elemental forces. Earth, air, fire, and water are not just components of nature; they are symbols, with each embodying unique energies and secrets that can amplify our manifesting endeavors.

ELEMENTAL FORCES IN HOLISTIC MANIFESTING

In intuitive manifesting, the natural elements—earth, air, fire, and water—aren't just symbols; they're dynamic energies that breathe life into our manifesting practices. Each one brings its own unique vibe, turning the process into this incredible, multilayered adventure of creation and discovery.

Earth provides the grounding force that anchors our dreams in reality. **Air** gifts us with clarity and creativity, allowing our ideas to soar and take shape. **Fire** fuels our passions and drives our actions, turning the spark of desire into tangible outcomes. **Water** bathes our practice in emotion and deep introspection, guiding us with its subtle wisdom.

Let's unwrap these elements and see how they energize our intentions.

Earth as Foundation:
Stability and Practical Realism

Earth represents the grounding force that anchors our dreams in the concrete world. It symbolizes stability and practicality, creating a place where clear, achievable goals are set and pursued methodically. Imagine launching a new business venture. Earth energy guides you in crafting a solid business plan, setting realistic financial goals, and meticulously charting the path to success.

In Tarot, the earth element aligns with the suit of Pentacles, which embodies wealth, abundance, and the manifestation of tangible outcomes. These cards remind us to ground our aspirations in the physical world, rooting lofty ideas in here-and-now reality.

Air as Clarity:
Mindfulness and Effective Communication

Air, with its ethereal presence, is like a fresh breeze for your thoughts, helping you communicate your desires. With air, you're engaging in a dialogue with the Universe, using your thoughts and words to shape your world. It's about tuning in to your internal chatter, making sure it's positive and focused. Aiming to boost your relationships? Air is your ally in expressing your needs and desires clearly, as you listen with empathy and understanding.

Air, with its light and elusive quality, breathes clarity into our mind, facilitating the clear communication of our desires. Engaging with air involves an active dialogue with the Universe, as we shape our reality through thoughtful words and ideas.

In the realm of Tarot, air corresponds with the suit of Swords, which represents thoughts and communication. These cards remind us to be deliberate in our mindset and self-talk, especially regarding our manifesting efforts.

Fire as Drive: Passion and Motivation

Fire, the element of transformation, ignites the spark of our desires, driving our actions forward. It embodies passion, energy, and motivation, which are essential in converting wishes into reality. Manifesting with fire means tapping into what truly excites and motivates you, channeling this fervor into your endeavors.

The suit of Wands in Tarot represents the fire element and symbolizes the "fire in the belly"—our motivation, passion, and desire to create. These cards serve as a reminder to pursue our dreams passionately and with zeal.

Water as Feeling:
Emotional Intelligence and Flow

Water, fluid and intuitive, brings emotional depth and intuition into play. It teaches us to harmonize our feelings with our goals as we understand and harness the power of emotions. Manifesting with water is emotional intelligence in action and ensures our dreams are not only fulfilling, but also resonate deeply with our hearts.

In Tarot, water is represented by the suit of Cups, which signifies emotional expression and relationships. These cards speak to how you express yourself, what you feel, and how you relate to yourself and others. These cards remind us of life's fluid nature, encouraging us to trust and follow our intuition on our manifesting path.

— ⬣ —

When these elemental forces intertwine in our manifesting practices, they create a harmonious and dynamic interplay. This balance ensures our manifestations are grounded, inspired by creativity, driven by passion, and in tune with our deepest emotions and intuitions.

The Tarot suits—Pentacles, Swords, Wands, and Cups—are invaluable allies on this journey, each resonating with these elemental energies. Their presence in our Tarot readings signals the active aspects in our manifesting practices. By embracing these Tarot energies, we deepen our connection to the elemental forces, which enriches our manifesting practice with a more intuitive and holistic approach.

Let's welcome these elemental forces in our manifesting efforts. Let the stability of earth, the clarity of air, the passion of fire, and the emotional wisdom of water guide us. As we blend these forces, we become masterful magicians, harnessing their combined power to bring our deepest dreams into reality.

It's fitting, then, that our Tarot Guide for this chapter is the Magician, a skillful balancer of earth, air, fire, and water. This archetype symbolizes not just power, but the wisdom to use it harmoniously. In the next section, we'll explore how embodying the Magician empowers us to masterfully weave these elemental energies into a cohesive force for transformation.

THE MAGICIAN: MASTER OF MANIFESTING

Meet the Magician, Tarot's number one, who symbolizes fresh starts and boundless potential. Picture him as a cosmic conduit, seamlessly bridging the ethereal Universe with our tangible world, channeling energy from above to below. He's a powerful reminder that we, too, have the ability to manifest our deepest aspirations into our everyday lives.

The Magician has the four potent symbols of Tarot—the Cup, Pentacle, Sword, and Wand—spread before him. Each of these represents the elemental energies of water, earth, air, and fire, respectively. This imagery serves as a reminder that the Magician possesses all the necessary tools to transform our intentions into tangible outcomes. These symbols aren't just for show; they're an

THE MAGICIAN

active call for us to tap into our diverse skills and resources to make our dreams come true.

The Magician's real trick? Balancing these elements. He doesn't play favorites; he understands that genuine magic is created when water's intuitive insights, earth's solid practicality, air's intellectual prowess, and fire's passionate drive converge. For instance, in elevating your career, the Magician's wisdom guides you to align your professional endeavors with your emotional truths (water), build them on a foundation of concrete actions (earth), strategize with clarity and focus (air), and propel them forward with fiery motivation (fire).

The Magician's Duality: Spiritual and Material Balance

The Magician also embodies life's duality—the spiritual and the material. He nudges us to remember that manifesting isn't just about material gains, but also about our spiritual journey and growth. This is about making sure that our real-world creations are in sync with our soul's purpose. Whether you're working on a creative project, launching a new venture, or on a path of self-improvement, the Magician asks: *Does this resonate with my higher self? Am I cocreating in harmony with the Universe?*

Manifesting with the Magician: Taking Inspired Action

Fundamentally, the Magician symbolizes the power of inspired action—the catalyst that transforms potential into reality. He reminds us that dreaming and planning must be accompanied by concrete steps. When manifesting, identify the action that will propel you toward your goal. It could be anything from writing that initial sentence to enrolling in a course or seeking a mentor. Actions imbued with the Magician's energy are not mere steps; they are quantum leaps toward realizing your dreams.

In essence, the Magician invites us to embrace a holistic approach to manifesting—one that intertwines the spiritual with the material and thought with action. As we tap into the Magician's balanced mastery of the elemental forces, we unlock the secret to turning our dreams into our reality—a testament to the transformative power of manifestation.

INTUITIVE MANIFESTATION IN PRACTICE: THE MAGICIAN'S TOOL KIT

Let's explore how to embody the Magician's qualities through daily rituals that work with the elemental forces of air, earth, fire, and water.

AIR: ARTICULATING GOALS AND POSITIVE AFFIRMATIONS

Start each day by writing down your goals and vocalizing them. Affirmations are key—choose ones that resonate with your objectives and dispel limiting beliefs. This practice sharpens your mental clarity, aligning your thoughts with your intentions.

EARTH: CREATING A SYMBOLIC ALTAR

Construct an altar with items that embody your aspirations. For instance, add coins or a gold symbol for wealth or a rose quartz for love. Let these objects be a creative and meaningful representation of your goals.

FIRE: VISUALIZING WITH PASSION

Engage in vivid visualizations of your goals coming to fruition. Feel the excitement in every cell, intensifying the energy and allowing it to radiate throughout your being.

WATER: RELEASING AND TRUSTING

Practice detachment from your goals, envisioning them as raindrops sliding down a leaf and being gently released. Notice how this fosters a sense of lightness and trust in the Universe's plan.

Tarot Spread for Elemental Manifestation

This spread is designed to provide a holistic view of your manifestation journey, incorporating the essential elements of earth, air, fire, and water. It encourages a balanced and mindful approach to manifesting your goals.

First, take a few deep, cleansing breaths. Then holding your Tarot cards, focus on your manifestation goal and intentions. Shuffle the cards and draw one card for each position in the spread below. Reflect on the messages and insights provided by each card and consider how the elements guide you in practical, clear, passionate, and emotionally intelligent ways. Use the guidance to take deliberate and empowered steps toward manifesting your desires.

Clarity (Air): How can I improve my mental clarity and communication to manifest my desires?

Grounding (Earth): What practical steps can I take to ground my intentions in reality?

Drive (Fire): What inspires and motivates me toward my goal?

Emotion (Water): How can I align my emotional state with the manifestation of my desires?

INTEGRATING ELEMENTAL WISDOM

As we close this chapter, I invite you to take a moment of still-ness and reflection. Consider how you can weave these elemental forces into your daily life and manifesting practices. Perhaps it's about setting realistic goals (earth), maintaining clear thoughts (air), kindling your inner drive (fire), or navigating with emotional insight (water). Each day presents an opportunity to balance these elements, enriching not just your manifesting rituals but every aspect of your existence.

Consider starting a journal to track the presence and influ-ence of these elements in your life. Observe how you can actively engage with their energies. Remember, the path of manifesting is a spiraling journey of intention, alignment, and action, driven by the elemental forces within and around you.

Looking forward, our journey will take us even deeper into the heart of manifesting—the realm of intuition. In the next chap-ter, we'll uncover how intuition is the very conduit through which cocreation unfolds. Intuition is our mystical link to the Universe, guiding us toward choices that resonate with the deepest parts of our being.

We will explore various techniques to enhance your intuitive abilities, which will empower you as a skilled cocreator of your reality. This journey is more than manifesting desires; it's about cocreating a life in harmony with your highest self.

∘ ◦ ○ ✳ ○ ◦ ∘

CHAPTER THREE:

The Power of Intuitive Manifesting

INTUITION IS SO MUCH MORE THAN SPORADIC HUNCHES or fleeting feelings; it's our most essential resource and an enduring wellspring of wisdom, like an inner oracle deeply interwoven within our essence.

I think of this inner wisdom as the soul's language. It doesn't speak in words; instead, it communicates through feelings, sensations, and those quiet but powerful inner nudges. Our intuition ties us to something bigger—a collective consciousness that transcends our personal experiences, allowing us to tap into a universal pool of insight.

Intuition shows up in many ways. It could be that physical shiver, goose bumps at a crucial moment, or that undeniable gut feeling that screams *yes* or *no*. Emotionally, it might appear as a wave of unexpected joy or a subtle sense of discomfort steering you in the right direction. And sometimes, intuition reveals itself in those moments of sudden, crystal clear insight when everything just makes sense.

To truly connect with this deep intuition, look for it in life's daily rhythm. It's less about crafted strategies and more about acknowledging and embracing intuition's natural occurrence. You'll find it in those quiet moments of introspection, like the clarity that comes from a walk in nature or the inexplicable sense of peace when a decision feels perfectly right. Intuition is our quiet ally, subtly informing our daily experiences. The more we recognize and value these intuitive hints, the more attuned we become to their profound wisdom.

Embracing intuition isn't about seeking it out through forced practices; it's about creating a welcoming space in our lives for it to be heard. It's a journey of becoming open to the soft guidance intuition offers, allowing it to be a key part of our decision-making. By appreciating these gentle cues, we grow in confidence, tapping into the unique wisdom that lies within.

Like Kathryn, who initially pursued a career as a nutritional coach. After a year of minimal client engagement, her intuition led her to her true passion: Tarot and astrological coaching. Now she has a thriving business she loves—all because she followed those intuitive nudges.

Or take the experience of Zoe, who was drawn by recurring dreams to the sacred rituals of ancient Peru. Heeding her inner call, she traveled to the Sacred Valley, absorbing shamanic teachings, and later returned to Australia to share this profound wisdom with hundreds of women through sacred retreats and workshops.

The science behind intuition is fascinating and adds a layer of grounding to the phenomenon. Neurological studies reveal intuition as an instantaneous, unconscious decision-making tool, deeply embedded in our limbic system—the emotional and memory epicenter of our brains. This rapid pattern recognition, drawing from our past experiences and environmental cues, is why intuition often feels so visceral.

Recognizing intuition as a blend of ethereal insight and logical reasoning enhances our ability to trust and utilize this innate gift. Intuition is a fusion of the mysterious and the rational, making it a dependable and potent ally in our decision-making. This understanding elevates intuition from a mystical whisper to a cognitive force and a trustworthy guide in navigating life's choices.

Intuition has always been a part of my life, from when I was young and could sense an angelic presence named Giant who watched over me to when I was a young adult and had prophetic dreams of a cheating boyfriend, and now as I act as an intuitive entrepreneur, teacher, and mentor to thousands of people around the world. But my personal connection with intuition played a pivotal role during the final days of my second pregnancy. When I was in my doctor's office at forty-one weeks' pregnant, the physician expressed concerns about the baby's size and floated the possibility of inducing labor. Pausing to tune in to my body, I felt a deep sense of well-being. Despite the enormity of my belly, my intuition whispered that my baby and I were in perfect harmony. "Let's wait a few more days," I suggested. "I trust everything is as it should be."

In the months leading up to this moment, I had been preparing. I engaged in practices that strengthened my intuitive bond—visualizing a serene birth, thinking affirming, positive thoughts, embracing trust and openness, and supplementing with acupuncture to ready my body. While I respected my doctor's expertise, my trust in my body's wisdom was paramount. It reassured me that all was well. While agreeing to further tests the next day, mainly to reassure my doctor, I had a strong sense that they would be unnecessary; my baby was nearly ready to make an appearance.

The following morning, while at the hospital for the requested tests, I felt the first signs of labor. A calm certainty enveloped me—I knew I'd return before the day's end. By late afternoon, what started as mild cramps escalated into the powerful surges of labor. As the sun dipped below the horizon, I was back in the hospital, fully immersed in the birthing process. The birth unfolded naturally, just as I had envisioned—without medication, without intervention, and as a blissful and empowering experience. And all because I trusted my body, my baby, and my intuition.

As we move forward in this chapter, we'll explore ways to enrich your intuitive connection. You'll learn to integrate intuition into your manifesting practices, tapping into its immense potential to lead you toward not just success, but deep, meaningful fulfillment.

HOW INTUITION IS AT THE HEART OF MANIFESTING

As we dive deeper into the world of manifesting, we find intuition isn't just a part of the process—it's the heart of it. Intuition is our internal compass and absolutely vital in steering us toward our truest intentions, ensuring our desires resonate deeply with who we are at our core.

Think of intuition as a bridge connecting your conscious goals with the hidden depths of your subconscious. It sheds light on what lies beneath your surface desires, ensuring your manifesting practice is as inwardly fulfilling as it is outwardly successful. For instance, when you're aiming for professional success, it's your intuition that nudges you toward paths that promise not just short-term wins but long-term fulfillment and purpose.

Take a moment to reflect on a significant decision in your life—maybe a career shift, a relationship, or a major life change. How did your intuition speak to you? Was it a gut feeling, a persistent thought, or maybe a deep, unshakable knowing? Pay attention to these feelings, as recognizing this intuitive guidance can enhance your trust in this inner wisdom, both now and in the future. The more you connect with your intuition, the stronger and clearer it becomes.

But let's be honest—tapping into and trusting our intuition isn't always a walk in the park. There are challenges, like the non-stop noise of our busy minds or the fear of trusting something so intangible. To overcome these, we often need to quiet our minds with practices like meditation or journaling as we learn to distinguish real intuitive insights from fear-based thoughts.

45

Our intentions set the course; alignment with our truths keeps us steady; and actions turn dreams into reality. Yet intuition is what weaves these elements together, ensuring our actions are not just effective but also deeply meaningful and truly aligned with who we are.

As we delve deeper in this chapter, we'll explore the essence of intuition and its pivotal role in manifesting a life that's not just outwardly successful but inwardly enriching. This journey is about reigniting a harmonious relationship with your inner oracle, trusting in its guidance, and leading a life of authenticity and true fulfillment.

TRUSTING YOUR INNER GUIDE

In the world of intuitive manifesting, your connection with that quiet yet powerful voice inside is precious. This inner guide, so often lost in the hustle and bustle of daily life, is the key to unlocking your most authentic desires and highest potential. Let me share a transformative story of one of my students, Dana.

Dana was a person plagued by indecision, constantly sweating over every choice, whether it was picking an outfit for a date or choosing between a downtown apartment and a suburban home. She'd loop through these choices in her mind, compile exhaustive pro and con lists, and seek out hours of advice from friends and even the occasional psychic. This process was draining—for everyone involved. And even when a decision was made, doubt haunted Dana, leaving her wondering about the paths not taken.

Then Dana discovered the magic of intuitive manifesting. She shifted her approach, turning inward instead of getting lost in overthinking. Meditation became her sanctuary—a place to quiet her mind. She explored her choices through visualization, feeling their essence. Journaling helped her unearth and dissolve limiting beliefs, and Tarot opened a profound channel to her intuition. This shift was monumental. Dana's world of turmoil transformed into one of serene, heart-centered clarity.

Her newfound bond with her intuition guided her to make choices that resonated with her soul, sparking significant changes in her life. Gone were the days of calling friends over wardrobe dilemmas; now, she tried on each dress and attuned to how she felt wearing it, choosing the one that was right. Decision-making became a journey of self-discovery. In just weeks, Dana had moved into her dream suburban home and began a relationship with a kind, loving partner who cherished her unique style. But beyond these external changes, she experienced a more profound inner revolution—a heart lightened by peace and connection, a spirit ignited by empowerment and gratitude. Dana felt calm, connected, and invigorated by life as she embraced the power of choice rather than seeing it as a burden. Her story became one of empowerment, connection, and joy—a testament to the transformative power of trusting her inner guide.

In my own journey and in guiding others, I've found that intuitive practices are profoundly transformative. They serve as a bridge to your subconscious, offering essential insights and direction. Here are some tools that have enriched my journey and those of my students.

Tarot Cards

Tarot cards are one of my favorite tools for connecting with intu-
ition. Having worked with Tarot cards daily during my entire
adult life, this beautiful intuitive tool is near and dear to my
heart. I have seen firsthand how Tarot cards have opened a path-
way to intuition in my own life and in the lives of literally mil-
lions of people who have engaged with my Tarot resources on
Biddy Tarot.

Tarot is more than just a deck of seventy-eight cards; it's a nar-
rative of our life, a reflection of our soul, and a key to unlocking
our inner wisdom. The Major Arcana cards narrate our spiritual
lessons, while the Minor Arcana reflect our daily challenges and
victories. I think of Tarot as the storybook of our existence, a mir-
ror to our inner being, and a gateway to our innate wisdom. Every
spiritual lesson we encounter is encapsulated in these cards. Con-
sulting Tarot unfolds the precise lessons needed for an inspired
life, like a mirror revealing our subconscious that allows us to tap
into the wisdom that resides within us all.

Unlike what you might see depicted in movies or TV shows,
the practice of Tarot is not about fortune-telling or predicting the
future. Instead, it emphasizes intuition over prediction, guiding
you to create your desired future and achieve your aspirations.
The true power of Tarot lies in using the cards to awaken your intu-
ition and inner knowledge, which makes it a perfect implement
for your intuitive manifesting practice. Connecting to your intu-
ition through Tarot can be transformative, leading you to positive
life changes and the realization of your dreams.

Engaging with Tarot is participating in a dialogue with your deeper self. This practice is not about seeking definitive answers, but about opening doors to your inner wisdom. Here's how . . . Create a sacred space for your readings that invites introspection. Hold your Tarot deck and set your intention or question. As you draw a card, see it as a peek into your subconscious, offering clarity and guidance. What symbols or colors stand out? How do they connect to your question? Avoid immediately looking up the card meanings; instead, let your intuition interpret the imagery and emotions that arise when you engage with the card. Over time, this practice deepens your connection with your inner wisdom.

If you're new to Tarot or just starting out, and perhaps feel a little daunted by doing a Tarot reading for yourself, don't worry, I've got you covered. I've created a series of free resources and tutorials to help get you started. Discover these techniques and more at www.biddytarot.com/imbook, where you can access free resources to begin your Tarot journey. Trust me: it's a lot easier to get started with Tarot than you think, and it unlocks so much potential for accessing your intuition.

Journaling and Writing

Writing, especially free-flow journaling, is a powerful tool for tapping into your inner voice. It allows your deepest thoughts and intuitive insights to surface. The act of writing can also be a meditative experience, deepening your connection with your intuitive self.

The magic of journaling lies in writing freely, letting your subconscious lead the way. Maintain a dedicated notebook for your intuitive journey, using preformed journal prompts or creating your own. Reviewing your entries over time can reveal patterns and insights, enhancing your understanding of your own intuitive language.

Journaling and Tarot cards work beautifully together, too. First, start writing in your journal. Then, when you feel like you have emptied your conscious thoughts, pull a Tarot card for more insight and journal for another five to ten minutes to go deeper.

Visualization

Visualization is a potent tool for aligning your subconscious desires with your conscious goals. It involves creating a vivid mental image of your desired outcome, filled with the emotions and sensations of its realization. By visualizing your desired outcomes, you actively align your inner self with your aspirations, which is crucial for effective intuitive manifesting.

Intuitive visualization is both a process of *creating* the vision (what you want) and *receiving* the vision (what your Higher Self or the Universe wants for you). So, at times, you might be watching the visualization play in your mind as you receive information from your Higher Self. And other times, you might be creating the visualization, turning it into what you are seeking.

To make visualization even more powerful, you can move from watching yourself in the vision (as if you were a bystander to what is happening) to being and inhabiting yourself in the vision (as if you are actually experiencing the vision now). Then enhance the vision—feel the feelings, see the images, hear the sounds, and make it even bigger and brighter. Doing this will trick your brain into thinking it is all happening now, in real time, and will amplify your ability to actually manifest your desires more quickly.

Throughout this book, I've included a number of visualizations to support your journey. You can perform the visualizations on your own, but I've found it's so much more effective if you listen to the visualization, allowing the words and images to guide your mind. I've made it easy with a series of free visualizations available at www.biddytarot.com/imbook.

Ritual and Ceremony

Rituals offer a tangible way to honor your intentions and nurture your intuition. These can be as simple or elaborate as you like, but their power lies in the act of creating a sacred space for introspection and connection. Use elements that resonate with your goals, such as candles, crystals, or Tarot cards, and make these rituals a regular part of your practice.

Start your ritual with a clear intention. Engage in activities that hold meaning for you, whether writing, meditating, or just sitting in quiet contemplation. Conclude your ritual by expressing gratitude and reflecting on how to carry the insights gained into your daily life.

Embracing these tools is about more than just adopting new practices; it's about opening up to a deeper level of self-awareness and connection with the Universe. Trust in these tools and your ability to use them, and watch as your intuitive manifesting abilities flourish.

These intuitive tools are what will put your intuition on speed dial, anytime you need it, throughout your manifesting journey. And as we dive into the Intuitive Manifesting Method ahead, we'll start to weave these tools into a step-by-step pathway for manifesting your goals.

Now, we're about to meet a guide whose wisdom is as deep as the mysteries she embodies. She's not just a figure in a deck of cards; she's the custodian of secrets, the holder of ancient truths, and a bridge to the profound connection between our inner wisdom and our ability to bring our deepest desires to life. She's the High Priestess, the Wisdom Keeper of the Inner World, shrouded in mystery yet brimming with insight. Let's delve into the secrets she holds, transforming our approach to intuition and manifestation.

THE HIGH PRIESTESS: KEEPER OF THE INNER WORLD

The High Priestess in Tarot emerges as a pivotal guide in intuitive manifesting. She embodies the essence of intuition, mystery, and the profound wisdom that resides in our subconscious. Cloaked in silence and sacred knowledge, the High Priestess beckons us to explore the depths of our inner world.

The High Priestess sits at the threshold of the known and the unknown, guarding the gateway to the deeper realms of our psyche. Her presence in your life is a call to embrace the quiet,

THE HIGH PRIESTESS

reflective spaces where true wisdom resides. She encourages us to look beyond the surface, to delve into the mysteries of our subconscious and trust the insights that emerge.

Perched at the crossroads of the known and the mysterious unknown, the High Priestess guards the gateway to our deeper psyche. Her presence is an invitation to embrace stillness and reflection, where true wisdom flourishes. She urges us to peer beyond the obvious, to dive into the depths of our subconscious and uncover the insights that await.

The imagery of the High Priestess in Tarot—the pillars, crescent moon, and crystal ball—is rich with symbolism. The pillars represent the gateway from the conscious to the subconscious mind, reminding us to travel between the realms as we navigate our daily lives. The crescent moon connects her to the divine feminine and the rhythms of nature, while the crystal ball she holds is a symbol of hidden knowledge.

This inward journey with the High Priestess is one of self-discovery. It's an exploration of our deepest truths, a confrontation with our inner shadows, and an acceptance of our whole selves. This introspective voyage teaches us that our deepest desires take root in the rich soil of our subconscious mind. Engaging in shadow work, guided by the High Priestess, allows us to confront and release fears, doubts, and past pains, clearing the way for more authentic and aligned manifestations.

The High Priestess also embodies the harmonious balance between masculine and feminine energies—a balance crucial for effective manifesting. She encourages us to blend the masculine drive for action with the feminine wisdom of intuition and natural flow. Embracing this duality leads to holistic and powerful manifesting in which we honor both action and intuition.

When the High Priestess makes her appearance in your Tarot readings, see it as a profound call to journey inward. She invites you to a place of deep meditation and introspection, urging you to listen to the subtle whispers of your intuition. This inner journey is vital for manifesting, ensuring that what you create externally is a true reflection of your innermost desires and wisdom.

Manifesting with the High Priestess

Manifesting with the High Priestess involves more than just realizing external desires; it's about an internal alignment with your deepest truths. It starts from within, from a place of understanding your subconscious drivers and aligning with them to manifest in the physical world. Nurture the seeds of your true desires—which are sown in the fertile ground of your subconscious—with the insights and wisdom you uncover.

As we work with the energies of the High Priestess, we learn to navigate our inner world with grace and understanding. We begin to see the interconnectedness of our thoughts, emotions, and beliefs and how these inner elements shape our external reality. The High Priestess urges us to explore these inner realms as we seek out the hidden wisdom that awaits us. In this sacred inner space, our true intentions are nurtured and brought to life, guided by the wisdom of our own inner High Priestess.

INTUITIVE MANIFESTATION IN PRACTICE: THE HIGH PRIESTESS'S REALM

Activity: Activate Your Intuitive Manifesting Powers

This visualization is designed to awaken your deepest intuition and supercharge your manifesting abilities. Perfect for moments when you feel stuck or need an extra push, this guided exercise will reconnect you with your inner power.

Close your eyes and take deep, calming breaths. Visualize a beam of radiant white light, a symbol of universal love and wisdom, descending from the cosmos. Feel this light enter through the crown of your head (crown chakra), illuminating your being with its celestial energy.

See this light flow down through your head until it touches your third eye chakra. You may even feel a warm, tingling sensation between your brows as this energy center opens, activating your intuition and unlocking your inner wisdom.

Allow this energy to flow into your heart, filling you with love, gratitude, and a sense of boundless potential. Feel your heart open, ready to embrace the endless possibilities of life.

Now, let this light descend into your belly, your center of creation and manifestation. Sense a profound connection as the light links your belly, heart, and third eye, uniting them in perfect harmony. In this state, visualize your dreams as if they are already a reality. Immerse yourself in this energy, absorbing the positive vibrations and reveling in the power of your intuitive manifestation.

Silently affirm to yourself:

I trust my intuition and welcome its guidance.

I release all doubt and fear.

What I seek, seeks me in return.

I am a force of manifestation.

When you're ready, gently return to the present, feeling empowered and aligned. Journal your insights or explore further with Tarot cards, deepening your connection with your intuitive self.

For a more immersive experience, download and listen to the free guided visualization for intuitive activation available at www.biddytarot.com/imbook.

As we wrap up this chapter on intuitive manifesting, let's reflect on our enlightening journey. Embracing intuition in manifesting opens doors to a world in which our deepest desires meet our authentic selves. The High Priestess, our mystical guide, has shone a light on harnessing this profound wisdom, highlighting the synergy between our conscious goals and our subconscious mind. By welcoming all aspects of our being, including our hidden shadows, we manifest not only effectively but with deep, resonating meaning and alignment.

As you continue to hone your intuitive manifesting skills, remember that this path is one of ongoing evolution and personal growth. Each step toward intuitive awareness is a step toward a more empowered, aligned, and fulfilling existence. So keep exploring, keep questioning, and most importantly, keep trusting in the profound wisdom that resides within you.

YOUR JOURNEY BEGINS NOW . . .

You are about to embark on a powerful journey to manifest your wildest dreams using intuition as your guide. And this is so special because not only are you using your rational, conscious mind to achieve your goals, but you are also using your intuitive, subconscious mind to align with your Highest Good and truly amplify your results. This is where the magic happens!

In part two, you'll learn the four essential steps of manifesting your dreams—from visualizing your ideal future and taking action that resonates with your soul to overcoming obstacles and amplifying your magnetic attraction. We'll also explore the transformative power of Tarot and intuition, as these tools can significantly speed up your manifestation journey.

And what's really cool is that not only is this going to help you achieve your own goals, but it will also show you how you can help others do the same. Imagine the incredible, positive impact you can make on the lives of those you love and serve.

This is a big deal—a turning point in your life—and I'm over the moon that you have said *yes* to this journey.

So take a deep, heart-centered breath; connect with your intuition; and turn the page. The Intuitive Manifesting Method awaits, ready to unlock doors to a life filled with alignment, purpose, and fulfillment. Let's begin this transformative adventure together!

∘ ○ ✳ ○ ∘

PART II:
THE FOUR-STEP
INTUITIVE
MANIFESTING
METHOD

We've arrived at the heart of our transformative adventure. Here is where we roll up our sleeves and get our hands dirty in the magical soil of cocreation with the Universe. We're moving from the what of intuitive manifestation to the how, from floating ideas to feet-on-the-ground action.

In the chapters to come, I'll teach you the Four-Step Intuitive Manifesting Method, which will be a game-changer in how you approach manifesting your dreams. This method is more than just a sequence of steps; it's a dynamic, cyclical journey that evolves with you, deepening your understanding of yourself and the Universe.

1. **Picture Your Perfect Future.** We'll start with a bit of day-dreaming—but the productive kind! Envision your ideal future. What does it look like? Feel like? Smell like? What does your intuition have to say about it? In this step, you'll get crystal clear on what you truly desire, designing a future that's in tune with your deepest values and truths and fully aligned with your Highest Good. This step is about creating a distinct and compelling vision, making your dreams so vivid and real that the Universe can't help but take notice.

2. **Elevate Your Energy Vibration.** Have you ever tried to tune in to a radio station, only to get static? That's what it's like when your energy isn't aligned with your desires.

This step is all about tweaking your internal frequency. You will learn to become an energetic match for your desires by raising your vibrational frequency to align with what you wish to attract, taking actions that resonate with your goals, and maintaining an energy that magnetically pulls your dreams toward you.

3. **Break Free from Limiting Beliefs.** Here's the part where we face those pesky inner critics. We all have them—those voices that say, *You can't do this*. Well, guess what? Overcoming obstacles is key to any process of change. This step focuses on identifying and releasing limiting beliefs and fears that hinder your progress. It's a cleansing process, clearing the path for your desires to manifest more freely.

4. **Supercharge Your Results.** The final step is about trust, surrender, and a whole lot of gratitude. It's about believing in the Universe's timing, being open to receiving, and amplifying your manifesting power through a mindset of gratitude. The more you celebrate what you have, the more the Universe will bring you reasons to celebrate. Enjoy your journey and the progress you've made, knowing that each step brings you closer to your goals.

Throughout these steps, we integrate Tarot and intuition. Tarot cards act as tools for reflection, revealing insights and guiding your path. Your intuition, meanwhile, helps you make choices that are true to your purpose. Together, they form a powerful duo, steering you in the right direction, ensuring your actions resonate with your soul's purpose, and enhancing your manifesting practice.

In the upcoming chapters, we'll dive deeply into each step. You'll get practical tools, Tarot wisdom, and intuitive insights to light your path. Remember, this journey is about more than achieving a one-off goal; it's about transforming how you interact with the world, how you align with your desires, and how you tap into the Universe's boundless energy.

Are you ready? Let's take our first step toward manifesting your perfect future.

CHAPTER FOUR:

Picture Your Perfect Future

ENVISIONING IS MORE THAN DAYDREAMING: IT'S AN empowering act and a deliberate crafting of your life's canvas. It's about diving deep, exploring not just surface desires but the profound aspirations that resonate with your soul. By dreaming *big*, free from the constraints of your current reality, you'll dare to imagine a future in which anything is possible.

Our first task is to broaden our horizons and explore all possibilities without restriction. I'll ask you to think beyond the boundaries of your current circumstances, beyond what you believe is achievable. If there were no limits, what would you create? This exploration isn't confined to material achievements; it encompasses emotional states, experiences, relationships, personal growth, and contributions to the world.

Once you've explored the vast landscape of possibilities, it's time to refine these dreams into clear, focused intentions. I'll show you how to harness the power of both your conscious and subconscious minds. Your conscious mind will help you articulate these intentions, while your subconscious mind, accessed through intuition and tools like Tarot, will ensure these intentions resonate with your deepest self.

The final piece of this step will be aligning your goals with your Highest Good, ensuring that your desires are not just about personal gain but also contribute to your overall well-being and the well-being of others. My students tell me time and time again that this is one of the most powerful aspects of intuitive manifesting and what truly made the difference in getting clear on what they most desire. We'll also work closely with Tarot as a powerful ally, as it offers insights that might not be immediately apparent.

Before we dive further into envisioning our future, let's start by uncovering our deep-seated desires.

DISCOVER YOUR
TRUE DESIRES

At times, what we think we want isn't always aligned with our true desires. We may yearn for a beachfront mansion or a sleek luxury car, only to discover later that they come with hefty maintenance costs or don't fulfill us as we had imagined they would. The Intuitive Manifesting Method asks us to explore our *core* desires—the deeper, authentic yearnings of our hearts. Unearthing these genuine desires often means delving into our subconscious, peeling back layers to access that more profound part of ourselves—the part that calls out for something more meaningful.

This is precisely where the power of Tarot and intuition shines. These tools help us strip away the superficial layers, revealing the underlying truths of our deepest yearnings. Through Tarot and intuitive practices, we uncover what we *truly* desire, moving beyond surface-level wants to the core of our being and a path of genuine fulfillment.

Our adventure starts by stretching the boundaries of our imaginations. Cast aside limitations and societal expectations; we're entering a realm where anything is possible. It's here, in this expansive mindset, that your deepest desires become more apparent and attainable.

Remember, not all goals need to be tangible or specific. In fact, we don't always know exactly what we want. That luxury car may look beautiful, but it requires a ton of maintenance—an expensive and ongoing chore—and though it rides like a dream, it doesn't actually bring fulfillment. Uncovering your true desire often

67

means breaking out of these kinds of specifics and allowing more room for your intuition to speak.

Even better, by allowing some spaciousness in our goals, we embrace the magic of possibility and invite the Universe to surprise us with outcomes beyond our imagination. This approach supports cocreation at its finest. Instead of manifesting a specific amount of money, you may choose to feel more abundant in your daily life. This opens up numerous ways to experience abundance beyond just a figure in a bank account. Or instead of manifesting a long-term, romantic relationship by a certain date, you may choose to experience love and connection in every new relationship you encounter.

Often, the most profound goals involve inviting certain feelings or experiences into our lives. For instance, aspiring to experience more fulfillment in your career or more curiosity in parenting can open doors to a wealth of unexpected joys. While these may seem like vague goals, they allow for greater flexibility and the ability to attract these feelings in various, possibly unexpected, ways.

The intention here is to get to our *core* desires, or what we really, truly want. This work often requires going down a few layers in our own subconscious mind, accessing that deeper part of ourselves. We want to unlock that yearning or calling that exists way beyond what we think we *should* want or what others might want instead. And that's why Tarot and intuition are so powerful during this step: they peel back those layers and allow us to glimpse the emotions underpinning our true desires. Recognizing and then recreating those feelings will be essential when it comes time to make ourselves an energetic match for our desires. By focusing on the *what* (the core desire) and the *why* (the feeling/emotion we want), instead of too much on the *how*, we allow ourselves that beautiful spaciousness, with lots of room for expansion and exploration!

Unleashing Your Imagination:
Broaden Your Vision

Let's move into that expansive place, shall we? We'll begin with a visualization and journaling exercise that will broaden the vision of your core desires. Create a sacred space for this practice, perhaps by playing soothing music, burning incense, or lighting a candle. Close your eyes and take a few deep breaths, imagining a beam of white light entering through your crown chakra, illuminating your path to self-discovery.

I invite you to go a little deeper here and listen to the Guided Visualization: Activate Your Intuitive Manifestation Powers. You'll find this free resource at www.biddytarot.com/imbook.

When you feel clear and connected, open your eyes. Now ask yourself, *In a world with no boundaries, what do I truly desire?* Let your pen flow freely as you journal for at least ten minutes, capturing every aspiration that surfaces, no matter how grand or minute. Allow your imagination to open the portal to your magnificent future.

Reflect on various facets of your life: relationships, career, wealth, personal development, health, lifestyle, and spiritual connection. Write down everything that comes to mind, and don't stop writing even if it feels challenging or hard—this is where breakthroughs often happen. Let your imagination truly take flight and open yourself up to all the possibilities that exist before you.

Next, turn to your Tarot cards for even deeper insights. Take a moment to tune in to your intuition. Then set an intention to connect with your deepest desires, shuffle your deck, and pull a Tarot card for each of the following questions. Remember, if you need some help with interpreting Tarot card meanings, look them up online or go to www.biddytarot.com.

As you reflect on each card, see what new information comes up about what you truly want in your life. You don't need to manifest every desire, but pay attention to the areas that bring you the most energy as you explore what is truly possible:

What do I desire in my life in general?

What do I desire in my relationships?

What do I desire in my career?

What do I desire in my finances?

What do I desire in my family relationships?

What do I desire in my health and well-being?

What do I desire in my home and lifestyle?

What do I desire in my spiritual connection?

What do I desire in my inner being?

What do I want to bring in *more* of?

What do I want to bring in *less* of?

What are my hidden desires?

Pay attention to the areas that energize you the most and note these revelations. Now, merge the insights from your journaling and Tarot reading. Review your top five desires and consider how they resonate with your deeper self. How do they make you feel? Are they exhilarating? Perhaps even a little daunting or scary? (That's okay—you're expanding your comfort zone right now to embrace even bigger possibilities.) Do they make you feel alive?

Beautiful! Next, you're going to connect with your innermost mind to seek out what you truly desire—this is powerful stuff!

Visualizing Your Future

You can trick your mind into believing your desired future is happening now—so time-travel into the future and bring that piece back to the present moment. The future becomes the now!

This happens when you visualize so vividly that your desired outcome seems completely real. You feel it in your body, experience the emotions associated with it, and see it unfolding before you. You become fully associated with the vision, planted firmly within it. This integration accelerates manifestation because it makes the future real and immediate.

So, with that in mind, here is a powerful meditation that will help you connect with your deepest desires, both present and future. After the meditation, jot down your insights, focusing on the symbol shown by your Higher Self—a guide for recognizing what matters most.

Find a tranquil space and relax. Close your eyes, take deep breaths. Feel connected to the earth and open to infinite potential.

Visualize radiant golden energy within you, with earthly support and universal possibility united.

See this energy expanding through your body and aura, representing your boundless potential. Invite spiritual guides, ancestors, and your Higher Self to join in, reminding you of your unlimited potential. As you sit in this light, let fears and doubts dissolve, replaced by radiant, multihued light from within.

Now, fast-forward to achieving your dreams. Absorb the details, people, emotions. Make it brighter, more real. Feel the joy, fulfillment, and peace of your goals achieved.

Focus on key areas of your life:

Relationships: Imagine yourself surrounded by love, deep connections, and meaningful friendships. Feel the joy these relationships bring.

Career: See yourself thriving in your career or business, achieving goals with passion and fulfillment.

Health and Well-Being: Picture yourself with vibrant health and energy, engaging in activities that nourish your body and mind.

Personal Growth: Envision embracing new experiences and opportunities as you evolve into your best self.

Feel gratitude for this life that is aligned with your desires. Let this vision permeate every cell of your being, knowing it's your future reality.

Finally, ask your Higher Self for a symbol that represents this future. Visualize it clearly. And even if this symbol doesn't make sense to your conscious mind, trust that your intuition is showing it to you for a reason. This symbol will guide your conscious mind toward what truly matters as you create your future.

When you're ready, gently open your eyes, feeling aligned and assured that your subconscious is actively shaping your future. Remember, you have the power to create the life you desire, guided by your intuition and inner wisdom.

If you prefer to listen to this guided visualization and go even deeper into your subconscious mind, you can download it for free at www.biddytarot.com/imbook.

Selecting Your Focus

Reflect on your top desires and the insights from your visualization. Then choose what you want to manifest—it could be one goal or multiple ones. Concentrating on a single goal can streamline your energy and potentially speed up the manifestation process. However, manifesting multiple goals can also work effectively, especially if they are interconnected and serve a common vision. The choice depends on your capacity to hold space for these aspirations.

Write your goal(s) down in your journal. Don't worry if your desire is not crystal clear yet; having an idea is a perfect starting point.

In our next step, we'll refine these desires into clear, actionable intentions, setting the stage for unfurling your dreams into your reality.

SET CLEAR INTENTIONS

Now you're ready to define your destination with precision and care. Unlike rigid goal-setting methods, we will embrace a more fluid approach, blending vision and emotion to set intentions that resonate deeply with your truest desires.

Setting clear intentions is essential because they serve as beacons, guiding your path toward manifestation. Vague goals lead to uncertain outcomes, whereas clarity in your intentions brings focus and direction. So much more is possible for you when you understand what you want to achieve, why it matters, and how it aligns with your Highest Good.

To set these intentions, engage both your conscious and subconscious minds. The conscious articulates your desires, while the subconscious taps into deeper layers, unveiling goals aligned with your Highest Good. This ensures your intentions reflect your innermost dreams.

Even if you've defined your desires already, it's important to revisit them at a deeper level. Each time you visualize what you want, you strengthen your ability to manifest it. You also receive more guidance about what your vision entails. This cocreation sets the wheels in motion while allowing the Universe to steer you toward the most ideal manifestation.

With your cards nearby, create a sacred space for this practice as you did on page 69. Center yourself through deep breathing or guided visualization as you did on page 71. Focus on your desire and ponder:

- **What would achieving this look like? Imagine the scenario's details.**

- **What will your life feel like after achieving this? Consider the changes that may occur.**

- **What emotions accompany this achievement? Note positive and challenging feelings.**

- **How will achieving this alter your identity and relationships?**

Visualize these scenarios using all your senses. Let your intuition guide you. Articulate your intention, writing it in your journal. Post it prominently in your home as a reminder of what you want to achieve.

Approach this process with lightness and trust. The Universe responds positively to this energy. Defining your destination is important, but there's still a vital step that many methods overlook.

The Intuitive Manifesting Method goes further, weaving your personal desires into the universal flow of energy. The next phase, which is unique to this approach, blends intuition, Tarot, and the Universal Laws of Manifesting to align your intentions with broader creative energies.

Trust the process. Let your intentions be the guiding stars. The path ahead holds discovery, alignment, and cocreation's magic.

ALIGN YOUR GOALS

Think of aligning your goals with your core values and highest potential as tuning a musical instrument. It's not just about hitting the right notes; it's about creating a harmony that resonates with your innermost self and the Universe's grand design. This fine-tuning ensures your goals are not only achievable but also enriching and fulfilling.

It's common to find ourselves at one of two extremes in goal setting—either playing it too safe or aiming for the stars. Imagine Vivian, who may set a small, easily attainable goal, only to find its achievement feels like a whisper in the wind, its impact on her life barely noticeable. Then there's Lee, who aims so high that his goal, once achieved, feels like a thunderstorm, overwhelming, unsettling, disrupting his life balance, and bringing more complexity than joy.

These misalignments often happen when we don't fully consider how our goals fit within the Universe's plan for our Highest Good. Remember, our aspirations ripple outward, affecting not just us but the world around us.

Attuning to Your Most Aligned Goals

Let's dive into an activity that tunes in to different versions of your goal, aligning you with the one that sings to your Highest Good. This exercise lets you explore the full spectrum of possibilities, finding the one that feels like a perfect fit for your true self.

Picture three versions of your goal: a cozy, within-reach version; a bold, step-out-of-your-comfort-zone version; and a sky's-the-limit, life-changing version.

Take a moment to feel into each version. What do you notice? What emotions come up? If you're feeling excited and energized, perhaps even a little scared, you're on the right track! If you're just feeling *meh*, then push the boundaries a little further. See how far you can take it.

Next, you're going to tap into your intuition to reveal which version of your goal is aligned to your Highest Good. Bring out your Tarot cards, and for each version of your goal, draw one card. Each card is showing you the potential experiences and energies of pursuing that version of your goal. The messages of the cards will guide you toward the version of your goal that's right for you. If you pull a card and its energy is not aligned with your vision, then take it as a sign that this version of the goal may not be for you. But if you pull a card and it feels completely aligned, then you have your green light!

Before deciding on your final goal, take a moment to check in on your feelings toward those goals again. Close your eyes and visualize each one. Notice the energy it brings. Does it spark joy and excitement, or does it feel heavy and daunting? What does this tell you about each goal and what is in true alignment with your desires?

Finally, combine your Tarot insights and intuitive feelings, and choose the goal that feels like a stretch, yet still deeply resonates with your Highest Good. It should challenge you but also seem clear and achievable. Write this chosen goal in your journal, making it a beacon on your journey.

One of my students, Ann, did this exact process and here's what happened. She initially thought a career shift to Tarot reading was her path to financial freedom and joy. However, when she pulled the reversed Star card while checking for alignment, it revealed a different truth. She realized this path would bring more disruption than harmony to her life. Ann realigned her goal and focused on expanding her existing career in school psychology. Within just a week, the Universe responded with unexpected opportunities, including a significant pay raise and a fulfilling connection with a colleague. And the cherry on top? Ann's passion for Tarot still found its way into her life when she was inspired to blend her love for the mystical with her professional work. That's a win-win for sure!

Aligning Your Aspirations with Your Higher Good

Aligning your goals is about more than just setting targets; it's about harmonizing your aspirations with your core values and the Universe's grand plan. It's about being open to the Universe's surprises, understanding that sometimes what the Universe has in store is even more splendid than what we had imagined for ourselves.

For example, if you're manifesting a new home, let Tarot guide you through different possibilities. Whether it's transforming your current space, moving to a new locale, or even securing a luxurious beachfront property, each option carries its own energy. Reflect on each option with your Tarot cards and feel into its energy, letting your intuition guide the way. Your final choice should resonate with you on a deep level, making you feel simultaneously excited and at peace.

Remember, your goals are living, breathing dreams. They can grow and change, just like you do. When I began my journey with Biddy Tarot, my goals were modest. But as I listened to my intuition and followed my joy, those goals blossomed into something far greater than what I had initially imagined. This expansion happened organically, driven by joy and alignment, rather than by setting overly ambitious goals from the start.

Stay open to the evolution of your goals. Sometimes, the journey of manifesting brings clarity and shifts in our desires. If a goal starts to lose its sparkle, it might be a sign to revisit and realign.

Aligning your goals with your Highest Good involves a blend of practicality, intuition, and trust in the Universe's wisdom. By finding this balance, you set yourself up for a manifestation journey that's not just successful, but also deeply fulfilling and in tune with the greater good.

THE TWO OF WANDS: THE SEED OF DESIRE AND INTENT

The Two of Wands emerges as a pivotal guide, embodying the essence of envisioning and aligning with your truest desires. This card perfectly mirrors the themes of this intuitive manifesting step: uncovering genuine desires, crystallizing intentions, and harmonizing goals with your deepest self.

Picture the scene on the Two of Wands: a figure stands within the secure walls of their castle, yet their gaze is drawn to the vast world beyond. This is the stance of a visionary—grounded in the

TWO OF WANDS

present but with eyes fixed on future possibilities. The globe in their hand whispers a powerful message: the world is brimming with potential and ripe for your aspirations.

The globe is not just a symbol of what could be; it's an invitation to dream boundlessly and to explore desires that stretch beyond the horizon of your current reality. The Two of Wands beckons you to dream without limits, to ponder your deepest yearnings without the constraints of what is clouding what could be.

And let's not forget the power of choice inherent in the Two of Wands. It's about selecting paths that resonate with your soul and making decisions that align with your true essence. This card is a gentle reminder that the choices you make now are the architects of your future.

Manifesting with Two of Wands Energy

To weave the magic of the Two of Wands into your manifesting practice, experiment with these approaches:

Visionary Contemplation: Stand in your present reality but let your mind wander into the realms of future possibilities. Give yourself the liberty to explore, to dream, to imagine what could be.

Embracing the Horizon of Potential: You're at the dawn of your manifesting journey. Greet the potential that lies ahead with open arms. Be ready to explore and discover.

Conscious Choices for a Resonant Future: Reflect on the paths unfolding before you. Which resonate with your core? The Two of Wands encourages you to choose with awareness, understanding that these choices are the seeds of your future.

Planning with a Dash of Boldness: While the Two of Wands is steeped in future visions, it also reminds you to balance action with thoughtful planning. It's about laying the groundwork for the daring steps that will follow.

Let the fiery energy of the Wands inspire you. Let passion, enthusiasm, and creativity be the fuel for your visioning process. Dream big and let your imagination soar.

VISION, MEET REALITY

As you continue on this path, remember that each step in intuitive manifesting is interconnected. The visions you've crafted, the intentions you've set, and the goals you've aligned—all these elements work together to infuse your core desires with the energy and vibrancy they need to materialize in your world. The upcoming step of elevating your energy vibration builds on this foundation.

So as we transition from envisioning your perfect future to elevating your energy vibration, carry with you the insights, revelations, and deep connections you've forged in this first step. The journey from envisioning to actualization is where the true magic of manifesting unfolds—a journey not just of achieving goals but of transforming and aligning your entire being with the Universe's abundant flow.

Embrace this journey with an open heart and a curious spirit. Let your intuition be your guide, your desires your compass, and your energy the vehicle that propels you forward. The path ahead is rich with potential and brimming with the magic of cocreation. Let's continue this journey together, turning your dreams into your reality.

CHAPTER FIVE:

Elevate Your Energy Vibration

NOW IT'S TIME TO ALIGN OUR VIBRATIONAL ENERGY WITH the dreams that ignite our souls. This chapter isn't just a step on your journey; it's a leap into the heart of manifesting. We are moving from envisioning to embodying our most cherished dreams. Here, we embrace the Universal Laws of Manifesting, particularly

85

the Law of Attraction and the Law of Vibration, as the heartbeat of our reality. These laws teach us that our thoughts, beliefs, and vibrational energies are powerful forces in sculpting our lives.

The Law of Attraction shows us the power of focus. Your thoughts and beliefs act like magnets, drawing similar energies into your life. Focusing on what you wish to create invites those experiences to unfold before you. Similarly, focusing on what you don't want attracts those unwanted outcomes. That's why getting clear about the positive outcomes you want to manifest is crucial.

The Law of Vibration works in harmony with the Law of Attraction, reminding us that aligning our vibration with our desires is key to bringing them into our reality. When you orient your vibration on what you want to manifest, you can bring it into your reality. And better still, when you join your vibration with your Highest Good, you reach new heights in what you can accomplish.

That's part of what we'll be focusing on in this step: elevating your energy vibration so you can become an energetic match for what you want to attract. When you vibrate at the same frequency as the thing you want to attract, everything flows much more easily and effortlessly.

And then, there's the Law of Action. This law is not just about doing; it's about doing with intention, with alignment. Actions that resonate with your desired outcome, infused with the energy of your intentions, are the ones that truly make your life sing. While visualization and positive thinking are important, they are not enough on their own. You need to take aligned action toward your goals to manifest them.

So let's turn our attention to the art of vibrational alignment, syncing our thoughts, emotions, and energies with our aspirations. When our vibrations resonate with our desires, the path to manifestation unfolds naturally, like a flower blooming effortlessly under the sun's warmth.

As we navigate this step, you'll learn how to become an energetic match for your aspirations. We'll delve into the philosophy of being then doing—first embodying the essence of your future self and then taking actions that resonate with this new state of being. Tarot will be our guiding light, helping you visualize and step into your future self.

THE SECRET TO MAGNETIC MANIFESTATION

Are you ready to transform your energy to mirror your grandest visions and meet your future self? Your future self is more than a distant dream; it's an imminent reality waiting to join you on this path of manifestation.

The key to magnetic manifestation is simple yet profound: *be* then *do*. *Be* the person you need to be to attract your desired outcome. Then *do* the things that fit to make it happen.

At its core, *Be Then Do* is about embodying the essence and energy of what you want to manifest before embarking on any action. It represents a major shift from the typical "do to achieve" mindset. Being then doing involves stepping into the future version of yourself, embracing the qualities, thoughts, and beliefs essential for manifesting your goal, and then becoming right now the person who has already realized your perfect future.

Let me share a personal story that illustrates this energetic shift. Back in 2016, my business was flourishing. I was generating a healthy six-figure income to support a fulfilling, balanced lifestyle with my husband and two daughters. Yet I felt an inner call to aim even higher—to elevate it to a seven-figure realm and help even more people connect with the power of Tarot.

Now, I'm naturally inclined toward action, so I plunged head-first into learning and implementing all the best online business and marketing strategies to rapidly grow my business. However, my results didn't match the frenetic pace of my action, and I was getting frustrated. As I voiced my frustration to my coach, she pointed out a crucial missing piece: I was doing all the right things, but I hadn't completely embraced the person I needed to be—a seven-figure CEO.

It was like someone had flipped a switch in my mind, sparking a 180-degree change in my approach. I shifted my focus to embodying the identity and mindset of a successful CEO, immersing myself in the feelings of flow, ease, success, and strong leadership. When I did this, I started thinking and behaving differently, making better decisions and taking more focused action that aligned with my goal of growing the business. For example, instead of spending hours every week answering every single customer email, I invested in training a new help desk team and freeing up my time to put my attention on growing the business and creating more high-value content for our students. This transformation from doing to being led to a remarkable change in my business, and within six months, I had doubled my income, achieving the million-dollar goal.

To truly manifest your goals, you need to upgrade your mindset to align with the future you . . . now. This must happen before you start to take action. You cannot expect change if you keep your mindset anchored in the old ways of being. If you take action from this old mindset, you'll continue to loop, creating the same outcomes you always have, rather than nurturing something new.

This principle of *Be Then Do* is laced through every facet of intuitive manifesting. Before taking action, deeply consider who you need to become to create the reality you want. Step into this future version of yourself, bringing all those necessary qualities into the now. This is when you start embodying the person who has already achieved your perfect future.

From this place of being, your actions become aligned and intentional. You act as if your desire is already a reality, because in the realm of energy and vibration *it is*. When your actions are born from this aligned state of being, they feel natural, effortless, and in flow. You're guided from within, with each step unfolding seamlessly as your path becomes illuminated.

In the pages to come, we'll dive deeper into how you can move into your future self and bring that energy to the present moment. I'll share techniques to align your energy and vibration with your desires, using Tarot as a guiding light.

BECOME AN ENERGETIC MATCH

Picture the Empress card in Tarot—she exudes a nurturing grace, and her presence is a symbol of potential and abundance. She teaches us, subtly yet powerfully, that to manifest our dreams, we must first become the living embodiment of those dreams. Our state of being—woven from our thoughts, emotions, and beliefs—sets the stage for our actions. To transform our vision into reality, we must immerse ourselves in its essence, much like an actor who becomes one with their role, blurring the lines between performance and real life.

I've experienced so many transformative stories of students who embodied their goals before bringing them to fruition.

Darcie, once an aspiring writer, transformed her dream into reality through the Intuitive Manifesting Method, particularly by embracing *Be Then Do*. No longer content with just *wanting* to be a writer, she shifted her mindset to *being* a writer right now. This profound change in identity marked a turning point for her. Embracing her new identity, Darcie began each day by asking, *What would a writer do today?* Her actions and decisions took on a new purpose and focus as she dedicated substantial time to writing her books, not as a mere hobby, but as her life's purpose.

Darcie's journey with *Be Then Do* brought her vision into the present, making it tangible and immediate. It led her to challenge the narratives she had about herself and her aspirations. "I don't want manifestation to be just something 'in the future'—I want it to be *now*," she reflected with me. This perspective allowed her to live her story, not just tell it. She shifted from a mindset of "I want to be a storyteller" to "I *am* a storyteller," actively creating her future rather than passively waiting or wishing for it. This approach turned her aspirations into a living, breathing part of her daily existence. She then forged a path where every action was a step toward fulfilling her true calling as a writer.

Becoming an energetic match to your desires begins with deep introspection and aligning with your spiritual essence. Suppose you aspire to enhance your intuition. In that case, you'll need to immerse yourself in the heart of intuitive living—embracing the mindset, resilience, and daily rituals that nurture a deeper connection to your subconscious understanding of the world. Picture your ideal day as the intuitive being you wish to become: the awakening thoughts, the books within reach, the practices and tools you use, and the inspirations that bolster your trust in your intuitive powers. Infuse this vision with life, feeling your intuitive channels expand with each passing hour.

For those seeking abundance, plant seeds of gratitude and generosity in your soul. If love is your aim, nurture self-love and empathy. Every day, perform actions that resonate with your chosen state of being. By consistently living these qualities and embodying them before taking action, you will calibrate your energy with your desires.

Remember, the mantra here is *Be Then Do*: it's not "do then be." This is not "fake it till you make it." Successful manifesting hinges on first embodying the person you need to become in the future and then acting from that place of alignment now. Consider the journey to a healthier lifestyle. Focusing solely on actions like diet and exercise without a mindset shift often leads people to revert to old habits. This happens because your actions are still driven by your previous mindset and not in sync with your new aspirations. For lasting transformation, you must first become—energetically— the fit and healthy person you envision and then make decisions from that identity.

The most rapid and profound transformations occur when you first embody the person you wish to be—in the present moment. From this place, you are then inspired to take actions that are truly aligned with this new version of yourself rather than your past self. This approach ensures that your actions are not just steps, but leaps toward becoming an energetic match for your desired self, leading to a life that resonates with your deepest aspirations.

Step into the You You're Becoming

Are you ready to *Be Then Do*, so you can indeed become an energetic match for what you want to create? It all starts with connecting with your future self. Who do you want to become? What does your future self look and feel like? And how can you bring those qualities, characteristics, and mindsets into the here and now?

Let's dive into some powerful techniques to embrace your *being*, starting with journaling and self-reflection. Here are two *big* questions to get you started:

- **Who do you need to become to manifest your goal?**
  Imagine the qualities you'll display when you've realized your manifestation. Will you be more courageous, nurturing, or decisive?

Feel into who you need to become. If you find yourself focusing on what you don't want, gently reframe it to what you do want. Remember, the Law of Attraction emphasizes clarity on what you desire, not what you want to avoid.

- **How would others describe you when you've manifested your goal?**
  What would people say about you? How would they perceive you? Maybe they'd see you as calmer, more grounded, or more focused. Take your time with this. It's a crucial part of laying the foundation for your success.

You might be called to close your eyes and feel into these questions. You may experience the emotions, hear phrases or words, or see who you wish to become. Allow your inner mind to speak with you in whatever way feels most enriching to you.

Then take ten to fifteen minutes to journal on each question. Keep writing, even after you feel like you have written everything. See what new insights arrive.

After reflecting on these questions, pull a Tarot card for each. Let these cards guide you deeper, inviting intuitive insights. Write your thoughts in your journal. Tarot often reveals unseen aspects of ourselves, so be open to what emerges.

To close out the contemplation, write in your journal, "I am . . ." and summarize who you are becoming as you manifest your goal. You might also include other prompts like, "I feel . . . " or "I love . . ."

For example, if you are seeking more health and fitness in your life, you might write, "I am strong, resilient, persistent, and

93

physically active. I feel alive, energized, uplifted, and sexy. I love nourishing my body with healthy, organic food and moving (and sweating) daily." Keep this handy, as it will be pivotal in the next step and the entire manifesting journey.

Then keep the channel open for the next few days or weeks, allowing new insights to flow to you. Meditate on these questions each day, reread your journal, and make sure you give yourself enough time and space to really go deep. You might even revisit your journal responses to see what new areas come up.

Be Your Future Self Now

You know who you need to become to manifest your goal. Now we're going to do a little time-traveling to bring that future self into the right-here-and-now self so that what you desire is no longer just a thing of the future but a thing of the present.

That's the beauty of intuitive manifesting: we can have what we want *now*. It doesn't have to be just something we wish for or long for. It can be something we can literally welcome and create now. By becoming aware of who we need to become, we start to realize that we could actually have or be that right here, right now.

So, going back to the example of attracting health and fitness into your life, as you reflect on who you need to become—strong, resilient, persistent, and a lover of healthy, nourishing food and daily activity—you realize that you can actually be this person *today*. You don't have to wait.

And as you start to be this person now, you start to manifest your goals much faster than you realized was possible. Because you've taken that future desired state and turned it into your current reality, you have become the future!

Let's make this happen. Go back to your journal and revisit what you wrote about who you need to become—where you wrote "I am . . .; I feel . . .; I love . . .; etc." As you read through your insights again, you will already start to feel that future self in your present self. But let's take it a little bit deeper and dial it up some more.

Close your eyes and take a few long, deep breaths. Now imagine yourself as the person you've become when you achieve your goal. Notice not just what you have achieved but who you are. How do you feel—physically, mentally, emotionally, spiritually? What do you look like? What are you doing? As you envision this future self, make the picture brighter, stronger, bigger. Feel the emotions, the sensations, the energy of this future self in your entire being. See if you can make it even bigger, stronger, brighter. Then, armed with this amazing future self feeling, picture yourself floating all the way back into this present moment, still carrying with you the qualities and energy of your future self, but bringing those things into the here and now. That's it. Imagine as if it is all happening now. You *are* these qualities right here. And imagine going about your day *today* with this new sense of self, this new identity, this new mindset. What will you do? Where will you focus your time, energy, and attention? Who will you connect with? Set your intentions and start making a plan for your day, now. When you feel ready, gently open your eyes and feel the magic of being your *future self now*.

I've also created a special guided visualization to help you align with your future self now and go deeper with this powerful exercise. You can download the audio for free at www.biddytarot .com/imbook.

Aligning with the future you needs to be a daily practice . . . now. Who do you need to become to achieve your goals? And how can you be that person *now*? Feeling is *being*. Feel it first. Be the feeling. Then do the doing.

Consistency is key. Show up every day and do the work. Imagine yourself *being* that person who is 100 percent aligned with what you want to manifest. Feel it as if it is happening *now*. Radiate the feeling: expand it; grow it. Then go about your day from this place. Look for evidence that the Universe is conspiring for your success. The signs are everywhere—you just have to find them!

MEET YOUR ARCHETYPE

Understanding how to be your future self is just the beginning—and this is where Tarot can help. As we've explored in this book, the twenty-two Major Arcana cards of Tarot are more than just images. They represent universal themes of the human experience, embodying spiritual wisdom and karmic lessons that can catalyze deep, lasting change. These archetypes are the living blueprints of human behavior. They are common patterns or models that subtly determine how we show up in the world. And these powerful cards can help guide your path to your future self in profound ways.

Picture these archetypes as wise, inner guides, shining light on the trail toward embodying the energy needed to manifest your goals. They're not just symbols; they're catalysts for insight and connection to your evolving self. By choosing a Tarot Archetype that resonates with your vision of your future self, you open new dimensions of understanding and relationship. This archetype becomes your guiding light, cheering you on and teaching you invaluable lessons that will enhance your intuitive manifestation journey.

With Tarot's archetypal wisdom at your fingertips, you can consciously bring the essence of your future self into the present, expanding that energy in more dynamic and effective ways and lifting your manifestations to unprecedented heights.

Activating Tarot Archetypes

Let's meet your Tarot Archetype and activate their powerful guidance and wisdom, shall we? For this activity, you'll need your Tarot cards and your journal.

Begin by laying out the twenty-two Major Arcana cards before you. (If you're not sure which cards they are, they are listed on the following pages.)

Each of these cards is a gateway to understanding the qualities you seek to embody.

As you look at the whole array of the Major Arcana, tune in to the cards that most resonate with your future self. You might be guided by your intuition—instinctively drawn to a specific card that catches your eye. Or you might review what each card represents and then consciously choose a card that aligns with your future self.

Whether it's the adventurous spirit of the Fool, the harmonious affection of the Lovers, or the courageous heart of Strength, let inspiration be your guide.

Here's a quick reference for the energies associated with each Major Arcana archetype:

0. The Fool—Curious, Spontaneous, Adventurous, Open, Fearless

1. The Magician—Resourceful, Creative, Powerful, Focused, Manifestor

2. The High Priestess—Intuitive, Mysterious, Wise, Inner Knowing, Reflective

3. The Empress—Nurturing, Abundant, Creative, Fertile, Sensual

4. The Emperor—Authoritative, A Natural Leader, Structured, Disciplined, Responsible

5. The Hierophant—Traditional, Spiritual, Teacher, Ritualistic, Knowledgeable

6. The Lovers—Loving, Connected, Consciously Aware, Harmonious, Values-Driven

7. The Chariot—Determined, Willful, In Control, Victorious, Driven

8. Strength—Courageous, Resilient, Strong, Compassionate, Confident

9. The Hermit—Solitary, Reflective, Wise, Guiding, Introspective

10. Wheel of Fortune—Adaptable, Optimistic, Open-Minded, Opportunistic, Adventurous

11. Justice—Fair, Just, Objective, Ethical, Discerning

12. The Hanged Man—Surrendered, Patient, Transformed, Reflective, Accepting

13. Death—Transformative, Renewing, Transitory, Accepting, Mystical

14. Temperance—Balanced, Harmonious, Patient, Moderate, Serene

15. The Devil—Tempting, Illusory, Provocative, Liberating, Self-Aware

16. The Tower—Changing, Chaotic, Liberating, Destructive, Revelatory

17. The Star—Hopeful, Inspirational, Calm, Guided, Faithful

18. The Moon—Intuitive, Mysterious, Emotionally Aware, Reflective, Connected with the Unconscious

19. The Sun—Radiant, Joyful, Vital, Confident, Empowering

20. Judgement—Awakening, Transformative, Redemptive, Reflective, Enlightened

21. The World—Whole, Complete, Accomplished, Integrative, Empowered

If you feel called to choose more than one card, go for it. But also remember to keep things simple and pick a maximum of three cards to act as your guides.

Reflect on your chosen cards. Why did each one call to you? What energy or transformation does each symbolize in your journey? This introspection is key to understanding how these archetypes intertwine with your personal narrative.

Dive into the essence of each card:

- **What new insights does the card reveal about the energy you need to embrace?**

- **Observe the symbols. How might they aid your manifesting journey?**

- **Envision yourself within the card. Are you the central figure, an observer, or something else? Experiment with different perspectives to unlock new understandings.**

You can even engage in a meditative practice with the card. Close your eyes, breathe deeply, and bring the card's image to your mind's eye. Step into the card, embodying its qualities and energy. What wisdom does this card offer you? Note down the insights and guidance you receive from this exploratory journey.

Place your selected cards where you'll see them daily. These cards are now your daily touchstones, continually reminding you of the energy you're embracing. Whether they're physical cards on your desk or digital images on your phone, let them be constant symbols of your alignment with your future self.

And throughout your manifesting journey, if you find you need insight, guidance, wisdom, or even just a little motivation, turn to these Tarot Archetypes. You might ask the card(s) for advice, intuitively channeling and writing their messages for you in your journal. Or you might meditate with the card and tap into its essence to boost your own energy and realign with your future self.

By forging a deep connection with your Tarot Archetypes, you're tapping into a wellspring of collective wisdom and unlocking profound insights within yourself. You're not just aligning with your goals; you're embodying the essence of your future self. And what naturally follows this state of being? Action.

TAKE ALIGNED ACTION

By now, you've started to realize within yourself the qualities and characteristics needed to achieve your manifesting goal thanks to your intuition and the guidance of your Tarot Archetypes. The magic in this process is that you've taken the crucial step of aligning your *being* before *doing*. If you had skipped this step—as many do—you might find things feeling hard and clunky or even going haywire as you attract unwanted outcomes and get further away from your goals. But you've focused on aligning your *being* first, so what comes next should flow easily and effortlessly.

Now, it's time for *doing* and taking aligned action from this new place of being. The neat thing is that because you have aligned your *being* first, the *doing* becomes that much easier and in flow. That's because it *is* easy when you are in true alignment. In fact, you might have already started to notice that the more you situate yourself in line with your future self now, the more you feel inspired to take aligned action. It just naturally flows. That's the magic—and why doing all the work of *becoming* is so worthwhile in the end, because it makes the *doing* so much easier.

When you are your future self now, knowing what to do next becomes easy. Simply step into your future self and ask: *What do I need to do next to bring my vision to life? What would my future self do now?*

For example, Kerry entered the Intuitive Manifesting program with a specific goal in mind: to accelerate the manifestation of an apartment in Paris for her three-month vacation—a plan she had been striving toward for some time.

First, she pictured her ideal apartment, getting very clear about what she wanted, from its appearance to its location, even down to the specifics like parquet flooring. Then Kerry started searching online for an apartment, and within twenty minutes she had found a place that matched her vision perfectly. She got chills!

But in the back of her mind, she worried it was too expensive. She worked with the Magician as her Tarot Archetype, channeling her future self as someone who had the resources to manifest their dreams and who could ultimately afford this beautiful apartment. She then meditated with this powerful Tarot guide, and the Magician said to her, "Take it! This is the one. You can do this!" So she did! She answered the Magician's call, trusting she had everything she needed to make this a reality, and booked the apartment. And she had the most wonderful experience in Paris as a result!

Now, notice that taking action doesn't mean creating a start-to-finish, cover-all-bases, step-by-step plan. Overplanning can actually box you in, as even the best-laid itineraries need adjusting when life happens! Instead, taking action means simply knowing the next step—just the *next* step. Because with each step, the one after will reveal itself with clarity and ease.

Think of this process like the Hermit card in Tarot. If you don't recall the imagery, take a look—it's such a beautiful card because the Hermit's lantern shines bright with his inner wisdom, illuminating the path for the next step only. He trusts that if he just puts one foot in front of the other, he will reach his destination through Divine Guidance. Each step directs the next, and the next, and the next. This, my friend, is aligned action at its best. We need to be more like the Hermit, taking everything one step at a time.

In my own experience, I used to plan my business twelve months in advance, knowing exactly which project I would work on each month. I even had an hour-by-hour plan for the next thirty days. Sure, I got a lot done, but there were also times when things didn't go to plan and went off track. Life threw curveballs—my kids got sick or my best friend made a surprise visit, and I had to reshuffle my calendar. Or sometimes I would be working on something that initially felt great and in alignment, but soon lost its shine, so I needed to take a new direction. Other times, my projects took longer than anticipated, and I needed to find more time to complete them.

I've since learned to be more fluid and flexible. I set intentions of what I'd like to create and I align with my future self. But instead of planning every step, I simply focus on my *next* step. I trust that all will happen within divine timing, that each step will lead me to the obvious next choice, and so on. I operate from a feeling of inner knowing, trusting that every initiative, every project, every task informs what follows and gives information about what to do next. Working like this means you shape the path as you go, rather than being locked into a defined track that can't be changed.

Students like Darcie, who we met earlier, and Debra have found their own ways to take the next step. Darcie made time to write a minimum of three nights per week and continued honing her Tarot reading and storytelling skills. Debra started by getting up every morning with resolution and living her days on purpose—a simple yet powerful routine.

Discover Your Next Step

So let's put this into action. It's time to discover what your next step might be. You'll need your Tarot cards and your journal. First, align with who you need to *be*—your future self. (Anytime you take action or need to make a decision to move further along your path, we'll always begin the same way—aligning with who you need to *be* before focusing on what you need to *do*.) Reread your journal responses and the exercises we did in the last section. Turn to the Tarot Archetype cards that you selected last time. Reflect on what you wrote. Remind yourself what it was like to step into your archetype card. Visualize who you have become when you achieve your goal. Embody this energy. Maybe you could add a mantra, a song, a picture, or a physical movement or stance to embed this even further. Take as long as you need to reestablish this connection with your future self.

Now, when you are ready, ask yourself: *What do I need to do next to manifest my goal?* Allow the answers to come in the most natural way for you. Maybe you want to meditate deeply to connect to your intuition, your subconscious, your Highest Good. Maybe you prefer to write about the question and record what comes to you in your journal. You might feel called to draw a few Tarot cards. You might even want to start by brainstorming all the possible actions you could take! These actions are different from a multistep, set-in-stone plan. The process helps to loosen the mind, revealing what's possible and bringing more clarity and confidence about how to move forward.

Whichever method you choose, come back to the simple question: *What do I need to do next to manifest my goal?* Then use your Tarot cards, intuition, and inner mind to guide you, jotting down your impressions in your journal. Now read through your ideas and circle up to five that feel the most impactful and aligned. Then choose one you can commit to *right now* . . . and do it.

Remember: when you take aligned action, go one step at a time. When you've completed that step, reflect on what you learned. Ask yourself: *What do I want to continue doing? What do I want to start doing? What do I want to stop doing?* Tune in to what feels good and in alignment. What doesn't? What does this tell you about your next step? Again, journal, pull Tarot cards, and open to your intuition through meditation and visualization. Then choose your next step. And continue doing this as you get closer and closer to your goal. It really is that simple.

If you take action and then get stuck, don't worry: it happens to the best of us! Just keep coming back to the simple question, *What do I need to do next to manifest my goal?* Use your cards, intuition, and inner mind to guide you. Remember to note it all down in your journal, because that is your written record and your touchstone for success.

As you start to uncover your next steps and aligned actions, you're likely going to also expose what doesn't feel like a fit. While it might seem sticky or uncomfortable at times, pay attention to these feelings of misalignment. As it turns out, what you *don't* do is just as important as what you *do* do.

Sometimes Aligned Action Means Saying No

Often, it's easy to say *yes* to doing more of what aligns with your goals: yes to new friendships that nurture your soul, yes to exploring hobbies that ignite your passion, yes to spending more time in nature that rejuvenates your spirit. These are the choices that seamlessly align with your journey toward your goals.

However, it can be more challenging to say *no* to what is no longer in alignment. This could mean realizing that a longtime friendship is no longer serving your growth and needs to be gently released. It might involve recognizing that certain habits, like consuming alcohol or sugar, are not in agreement with your goals for a healthy lifestyle and, thus, need to be let go.

Making these changes can sometimes cause a wobble in your manifesting journey. It may feel uncomfortable at first, as you start to implement these changes. Others might notice this transformation in you and, instead of offering support, question your actions. This is a natural part of the process as you become more attuned to what truly serves your Highest Good.

In reality, what you're doing is getting super-clear about what you will and won't allow in your life and what actions you will and won't take. This clarity is essential for staying true to your path and ensuring that your every move is in alignment with your ultimate goals.

This process of discernment—of saying *yes* to what aligns and *no* to what doesn't—is a powerful tool in your manifesting journey. It ensures that your energy is invested in actions and relationships that truly resonate with your goals, helping you to manifest your desires with greater ease and clarity.

THE TEN OF CUPS—ALIGN WITH YOUR FUTURE BLISS

The Ten of Cups paints this idyllic picture—a happy family dancing underneath a rainbow together next to their perfect home. It represents everything you could ever dream of—and more! This is your bliss!

In this scene, a couple stands, arms open, embracing their world with their child nearby. Each Cup in the rainbow symbolizes an aspect of a fulfilled life: love, stability, joy. This card is not just an image; it encapsulates true, everlasting love and everything one could wish for—a home, family, and above all, a deeply fulfilling connection with loved ones.

Every symbol in the Ten of Cups speaks volumes. The family home represents comfort and stability. The hills symbolize fertility and growth. The rainbow is a divine promise—a herald of good times after the storm, assuring us that all will be well.

TEN OF CUPS

The Ten of Cups truly represents your ideal future, the kind that will bring you so much joy and contentment. It's one of the most positive and uplifting cards in the Tarot deck, representing true emotional fulfillment, happiness, and lasting bonds.

The magic of this card is being able to feel into this joy and happiness every day, as if it's happening right now. As you mentally place yourself in this idyllic scene, let the bliss and fulfillment of your perfect future wash over you. This card encourages you not just to dream of this state but to feel it in your being *now*.

In this way, the Ten of Cups reminds us of our present completeness. It tells us that while we aspire toward future goals, we must not overlook the wholeness we possess already. It encourages us to tap into this sense of completion, achievement, and fulfillment every day.

Manifesting with the Ten of Cups' Energy

Here's how you can work with the Ten of Cups' powerful, loving energies:

Visualize Your Perfect Future. Envision the life that fills you with joy and happiness. See the loving relationships, the heartfelt connections, and the personal achievements.

Feel the Joy Now. Embrace the bliss of your dreams as if they are your current reality. Let this happiness resonate in you today.

Celebrate Current Blessings. Acknowledge the aspects of your ideal future that are already present in your life. Gratitude is a powerful tool in bridging the gap between the reality of now and your dreams.

Embrace Wholeness. Focus on what you have, not what you lack. Recognize your progress toward your goals and cherish your current state of being.

Follow Your Heart and Intuition. Let your emotions guide your path. If something feels right, pursue it with passion; if it does not, reconsider your direction. Align your actions with your deepest values, not with external expectations.

The Ten of Cups encourages following your intuition to create more love, joy, and connection in your life. When something feels good and fully aligns with your values, do more of it. This card reminds you that you already possess deep inner wisdom. By listening and surrendering to it, your feelings will guide you along the path to profound fulfillment. You have the power to build your own Ten of Cups life by staying true to your heart.

"I AM WHOLE" RITUAL

This meditation and ritual remind you that you are indeed whole and that tapping into wholeness is what will help you embody your future self now.

In your mind's eye, picture yourself in the future when you have successfully achieved your goal. What are you doing? Who have you become? (This will get easier for you the more you engage with it. This type of repetition becomes so powerful *because* you are so good at it, enhancing your manifestations every time you do.) Now take a moment to feel into the sensations of wholeness that arise, knowing that you *are* everything you imagined and you *have* everything you imagined. Feel that sensation of wholeness in every cell of your body—that's it. Now picture the feeling of wholeness as if it is a ball of energy that you are holding in your hands. Notice the color, the size, and the brightness of this ball.

Imagine yourself traveling through time back to the present moment, holding this ball of wholeness in your hands. Notice how it continues to shine bright and strong as you travel all the way back to now. As you sense yourself arriving in the present moment, look down at your ball of light and feel the light permeating into your body and your energy field, filling you with a sense of wholeness right in the present moment.

Say quietly to yourself, *I am whole. I am complete. I am my future self—now.* Repeat this two more times.

Open your eyes, and if you feel called to, journal any insights and pull cards. You may like to ask Tarot, "In what ways am I already whole?" and "In what ways do I already embody my future self?"

Repeat this ritual anytime you wish to tap into the energy of the Ten of Cups and reconnect to your wholeness and bliss.

Remember: the path of intuitive manifestation is not just about *reaching a destination*; it's about *evolving and growing* along the way. Each step you take, each challenge you overcome, brings you closer to not only achieving your goals but also to becoming the person who effortlessly manifests their desires. Keep this spirit of growth and resilience with you as you continue on this exciting path.

CHAPTER SIX:
Break Free from Limiting Beliefs

DESPITE OUR BEST INTENTIONS, THE PATH TO MANIFESTING our grandest visions is rarely a straight line from *A* to *B*. Just like when you travel a winding mountain road, it's natural to encounter twists, bumps, and occasional dead ends along the way. And while setbacks can be disheartening in the moment, these challenges offer you invaluable opportunities for self-discovery and growth.

In this chapter, you'll learn how to break through these challenges. From shaking off limiting beliefs to managing impatience, you'll discover how to clear away what's no longer serving you so you can swiftly realign when life throws you off course. Confronting these barriers head-on not only empowers you as you pursue your present goals; it also equips you for all future endeavors. You'll emerge ready to manifest freely and confidently, unencumbered by doubt and resistance.

Sara, one of my students, knows this story all too well. Her leap from an agency copywriter to a thriving herbalist is nothing short of transformative, and the story of how she did it is a tale brimming with self-discovery and empowerment. Despite her undeniable talent and deep-seated aspirations, Sara found herself repeatedly buffeted by life's curveballs—a car that just wouldn't start, bills popping up like unwelcome guests—with each challenge seemingly chaining her to her current job.

But here's where the magic happens: Sara's true breakthrough surged forth when she consulted her Tarot cards and connected with her intuition. What she discovered was a deeply rooted belief that earning money from plant healing was somehow "wrong." Once this barrier had been exposed to her conscious awareness, Sara immediately got to work courageously challenging and reshaping this belief. She painted a new vibrant vision in which she could both heal others and be rightfully compensated. And as a result, Sara blossomed into a successful herbalism business owner.

This story isn't just Sara's; it mirrors a universal experience of those with the burning desire for transformation: our dreams are often tempered by the whispers of our own inner critics. Manifesting your grandest visions isn't just about directing your focus toward them; it's equally about addressing the undercurrents of doubt, fear, and self-limitation that rise to the surface along the way.

I think of these internal challenges as crossroads, where your response shapes your journey. Ignoring these feelings can seem like a good fix, but much like shadows, feelings tend to stretch longer and become more daunting over time. On the other hand, confronting them head-on, acknowledging their presence, and then consciously choosing to release these limiting beliefs are what truly empowers you.

This chapter is your map to identifying and outsmarting common blockages in the manifesting process. You'll learn to spot and shake off limiting beliefs and doubts, manage the drumbeat of impatience, and sidestep life's unexpected detours. We'll also spotlight inertia and procrastination, and you'll learn strategies to ensure you stay on track even when they crop up. By the end of this chapter, you'll be armed with a crystal clear, aligned strategy to dissolve any barriers that dare block the way of your manifesting success.

Freeing yourself from limiting beliefs is a game-changer at any stage of your manifesting journey. Blocks can pop up out of nowhere, and being ready to face them head-on is crucial to your success. Tackling these blocks aligns your conscious desires with your subconscious beliefs, and when these are in sync, manifesting becomes a seamless, joyful process.

Confronting these blockages sends a resounding message to your subconscious: *I am a force of nature—adaptable, resilient, and capable of bouncing back from any setback.* This mindset does more than empower you in the now; it strengthens you for future manifesting endeavors.

So what types of blocks might try to trip up your manifesting goals? As we've seen in Sara's story, limiting beliefs can be a formidable foe. Now, let's look into the most common obstacles in manifesting and discover how you can soar above them.

THE FIVE BLOCKS OF MANIFESTING

It's time to uncover and conquer the sneaky obstacles that can subtly derail our dreams. These blocks, often hidden just beneath the surface, can be formidable foes in our quest to bring our desires to life. Let's examine the five primary blocks of manifesting and discover how they might be craftily influencing your journey.

Block 1: Limiting Beliefs

Just like Sara's belief about earning from plant healing, your own limiting beliefs, whether glaringly obvious or lurking in the shadows of your subconscious, can act as invisible anchors. These preconceptions might whisper that more income means less time with family or that you don't deserve success. They're sneaky, creating barriers that disrupt the flow of your positive, manifesting energy.

Block 2: Fear and Doubt

Fears and doubts can build a wall of resistance within you. Whether you're experiencing the fear of failure or of success, these emotions, especially during setbacks, can cast a long, dark shadow over your goals. Thoughts like *Can my business really hit six figures?* or *Is love still in the cards for me?* are the echoes of these deep-seated anxieties.

Block 3: Procrastination and Inaction

Starting with a burst of enthusiasm but gradually losing momentum can lead to procrastination and inaction. When you stop aligning your energy with your goals, the path can start to feel insurmountable, leading to a frustrating standstill.

Block 4: External Influences and Setbacks

External factors like negative feedback, distractions, or unforeseen barriers can throw a wrench in the works of your manifestation efforts. Discouraging words from others or unexpected hurdles can challenge your ability to maintain a positive and focused vision on your goals.

Block 5: Lack of Patience

Manifestation is not a sprint; it's a marathon—a test of patience and endurance. Impatience can lead to frustration, which sends your energy veering off course. Remember, manifestation unfolds over time, and craving immediate results can disrupt this magical process.

Do you see yourself in any of these blocks? Whether you're facing one or several, it's a completely normal part of the manifesting process. The key is to pinpoint your specific blocks.

To unearth your blocks, dive into reflective journaling or consult your Tarot cards for deeper insights. Ask yourself:

- **What obstacles are hindering my manifesting journey?**

- **Where is resistance creeping into my life?**

- **Which limiting beliefs are lurking on my path?**

- **How can I kick-start the process of releasing these limitations?**

Identifying your blocks is just the start. What comes next is crucial. These blocks call for thoughtful, creative strategies to overcome them. And don't worry—you're not on this journey alone. In the following sections, we'll dive deeply into how to tackle these blocks, and I'll equip you with the tools and insights necessary to transform these challenges/blocks into opportunities, sending you toward manifesting success.

LIMITING BELIEFS

Limiting beliefs, whether they're fluttering around in your conscious mind or hiding in the depths of your subconscious, can significantly shape your life. Illuminating these beliefs and bringing them into the radiant light of conscious awareness are transformative steps in reshaping them and, in doing so, pointing a spotlight on the path to positive manifestation.

118

Reflect on the Law of Vibration, which highlights the magic of aligning your energy with your aspirations. If your focus is on what you lack or what you think you can't achieve, you'll inadvertently attract more of the same. In contrast, concentrating on your strengths and possibilities draws you closer to realizing your goals, like a magnet pulling you toward your dreams.

As Beth, one of my students, shared, "Clearing my limiting beliefs helped to create more space for positive thoughts and allowed my vision to come to life with joyful anticipation. And it wasn't just a one-and-done thing—I needed to consistently deal with each limiting belief as it came up so as not to block my manifesting mojo."

Let's explore some common limiting beliefs that might be stealthily impeding your manifesting:

Self-Worth Beliefs: Negative thoughts about your worth, such as *I'm not worthy of success* or *I don't deserve happiness*, can erode your confidence and obstruct your manifesting abilities.

Abundance Beliefs: Holding on to beliefs like *Money is hard to come by* or *There's never enough* fosters a scarcity mindset, effectively blocking the flow of abundance into your life.

Beliefs About Limitations: Convincing yourself of limitations, with thoughts like *I'm not talented enough* or *I'm too old to start something new*, can severely restrict your potential and opportunities.

Beliefs About Failure: Fear of failure, encapsulated in thoughts like *Failure is shameful*, can paralyze your progress and stifle your growth.

Beliefs About Others' Opinions: Concerns over others' judgments or the need for their approval can limit your authenticity and prevent you from taking actions that align with your true desires.

Beliefs About Change: Resisting change with ideas like *Change is always difficult* creates a barrier to embracing new possibilities and opportunities.

Beliefs About Success: Believing that *Success only comes to the lucky few* erects unnecessary barriers to achieving your goals.

You might already be aware of some of these limiting beliefs in your life. Or, perhaps, this discussion is bringing them to your conscious awareness for the first time. Often, these ideas are subtly ingrained in our subconscious, shaped by factors such as upbringing, societal norms, and past experiences. Drawing them into conscious awareness is the first step in transforming them.

Release Your Limiting Beliefs

Releasing your limiting beliefs is a transformative process that not only changes how you view your goals but also reshapes your entire approach to manifesting.

STEP 1: UNCOVER YOUR LIMITING BELIEFS

Start by confronting the reasons you believe you can't achieve your goal. This is a safe space for honesty—let out every worry, fear, and doubt without judgment. Reflect on the types of limiting beliefs we've discussed and see which ones resonate with you.

Use your Tarot cards to delve deeper, asking, "What other limiting beliefs do I have?" This will help bring any subconscious beliefs to the surface.

STEP 2: CHALLENGE AND DISPROVE YOUR BELIEFS

Now, for each belief you've identified, actively seek out reasons why it's not true. Look for evidence that contradicts these beliefs. Challenge yourself with questions like:

- **Is this belief genuinely true?**

- **How can I prove this belief wrong?**

- **What would a supportive friend say about this belief?**

Turn to your Tarot cards for additional insights, allowing them to guide you in understanding why these beliefs are unfounded.

STEP 3: TRANSFORM BELIEFS INTO POSITIVE AFFIRMATIONS

Take each limiting belief and turn it around into a positive, empowering affirmation. Reflect on questions that promote a supportive mindset:

- **What positive belief can I adopt instead?**

- **How can I reframe this belief to be more constructive and beneficial?**

- **What would an encouraging mentor say to convince me of my capabilities?**

Adjust each affirmation until it resonates with you, feeling authentic and believable.

STEP 4: REASSESS AND RELEASE

Return to your list of beliefs and reconsider how you feel about each one. Some beliefs may have lost their hold, while others might need further attention.

For persistent beliefs, use the following Tarot spread for deeper exploration and release. Draw a card for each question and reflect on how it aids you in overcoming your limiting beliefs.

1. **What is the limiting belief that is holding me back?**

2. **What is the impact of maintaining this belief?**

3. **What can I do to release this belief?**

4. **What is possible when I release this belief?**

— ◁◯▷ —

Regularly identifying, challenging, and releasing new limiting beliefs make up a practice that keeps your path to manifesting clear and unobstructed. This ongoing process is not just about achieving specific goals; it's about evolving into a person who manifests with ease, confidence, and a deep sense of self-awareness.

Colleen, an intuitive healer and Reiki practitioner, overcame her doubts about her business acumen. She refocused on her qualifications and the transformative impact she has on her clients, leading her to attract three new clients in a short time.

Barry shifted his belief that he needed more training before he could pursue his dream career and instead reminded himself that he was already in a position to share his wisdom and experience with others.

By embracing these steps for releasing limiting beliefs, you're engaging in the profound work of self-discovery and transformation. You're not just addressing the superficial layers; you're excavating the very core of what holds you back, reshaping your mindset, and paving the way for a successful and fulfilling manifestation journey.

DEALING WITH DOUBT

Doubt may be a familiar shadow in our lives, but it doesn't have to be a stumbling block. Instead, let's transform doubt into a powerful catalyst for growth and confidence. Take inspiration from Georgina's journey: "I often find myself doubting my decisions, questioning if they're right. My goal is to cultivate trust in my judgment and accept that it's okay to be wrong sometimes."

Let's explore strategies to navigate doubts and harness their energy for a positive, transformative journey.

Embrace the Universality of Doubt. Recognize that doubt can emerge at any stage of your manifesting journey. There might be doubt about the goal you've chosen, your ability to achieve it, or the effectiveness of your actions. Doubt often arises when you are facing new challenges or moving beyond your comfort zone.

Understanding its universality helps you see doubt as a natural part of growth and an experience shared by all who dare to dream big.

Observe Doubt Without Judgment. When doubt surfaces, approach it with curiosity rather than judgment. Acknowledge it as your mind's natural response to change. By observing doubt without letting it define you, you reduce its influence over your actions and decisions. It's like watching clouds pass in the sky—they're there, but they don't have to overshadow your sun.

Reflect on Your Successes. Think back to times when you've overcome doubt and achieved your desires. This reflection is a powerful reminder of your power to move past doubt, reinforcing your trust in your own abilities. It's like flipping through a scrapbook of your victories, with each one a testament to your strength and resilience.

Seek Positive Reinforcement. Actively look for signs that the Universe is supporting you. Focus on the progress you're making and the aspects of your manifesting that are going well. This positive focus helps overshadow doubts and reinforces your belief. It's like collecting evidence of the Universe's encouragement.

Embody Courage and Strength. Cultivate feelings of bravery and resilience. Connect with the Tarot Archetypes of Strength or the Chariot, drawing inspiration from their energies. Visualize yourself embodying these qualities, allowing them to guide and empower your actions. Imagine donning a cloak of courage and being ready to face any challenge with a heart full of bravery.

Act Despite Doubt. Remember, action is a powerful antidote to doubt. Taking steps forward, even when doubt is present, builds confidence and clarity. Each action you take reinforces your commitment to your goals and helps dissipate lingering doubts. It's like walking through a misty forest; with each step, the path becomes clearer and your destination more certain.

By embracing these strategies, you can transform doubt from a speed bump to a stepping stone on your path to manifesting your dreams. Doubt, when navigated wisely, becomes an opportunity for personal growth and a testament to your evolving manifesting prowess. It's a journey of turning uncertainty into a dance of empowerment, in which each moment of doubt conquered is a step closer to your dreams.

PUSH THROUGH PROCRASTINATION

While procrastination can certainly slow you down, it doesn't have to be a roadblock. See it more like a signal, indicating a need for realignment or a pause for reflection. Recognizing and acknowledging this tendency toward procrastination is your first empowering step toward overcoming it.

Procrastination often springs from a few key sources:

- **Lack of Motivation:** This happens when your goals don't deeply resonate with you. It's crucial to infuse your goals with personal meaning and visualize their transformative impact on your life.

- **Perfectionism:** When you set sky-high standards, the fear of not meeting them can lead to delays. Aim for realistic, achievable goals to sidestep the perfectionism trap.

- **Overwhelm:** Facing a mountain of tasks can freeze you in your tracks. Focus on one step at a time to melt away any anxiety about what to do next.

- **Limiting Beliefs:** As we've explored, doubts about your capabilities can lead to procrastination. Continuously work on releasing these negative beliefs to liberate yourself from this cycle.

If you find yourself losing focus on your grand goals, consider what is lying beneath that. Keep in mind that, sometimes, procrastination may be a sign that you are off course or not fully committed to your goal. Use this as a golden opportunity to reassess and realign with your true intentions.

Strategies to Overcome Procrastination

To reignite your manifesting fire, try these strategies:

- **Practice Self-Forgiveness.** Wipe the slate clean. Forgive yourself for past detours and focus on the now.

- **Reflect on Your Goals.** Revisit the why behind your goals. This can rekindle your motivation and sharpen your focus.

- Break Down Goals. Large ambitions can be daunting. Slice your goals into smaller, manageable tasks to make progress feel within reach.

- Prioritize and Manage Time. Assess your commitments and put those that align with your goals first. Schedule time in your calendar so you can channel your time and energy toward what matters most.

- Take Small Actions Consistently. Commit to regular, bite-size actions. Consistency is the magic key to maintaining momentum.

- Learn from Setbacks. Embrace setbacks as lessons. Analyze them for insights and growth opportunities.

- Seek Support and Accountability. Share your goals with those who can offer support and hold you accountable.

To gain deeper insights and overcome procrastination, I invite you to consult this Tarot spread:

1. Where am I now in relation to my goal?

2. How can I practice self-forgiveness and acceptance?

3. What lessons can I learn from past setbacks?

4. What do I need to release to move forward?

5. What actions can I take to create an optimal environment for manifesting my goals?

INTUITIVE MANIFESTING

Record your insights and revisit them regularly. And if you get stuck again, come back to this Tarot reading as inspiration for creating momentum again.

Remember: encountering setbacks is a natural part of any journey. The magic lies in how you respond to them. Keep revisiting your goal, reconnecting with your aligned energy, and reminding yourself that life's challenges are opportunities for growth and learning. Armed with these tools and strategies, you're well-equipped to tackle procrastination and inaction, staying firmly on the path to manifesting your dreams.

DEALING WITH SETBACKS

You've been a beacon of alignment and resilience, overcoming doubts and staying true to your path. And yet it's still not uncommon to find yourself momentarily sidetracked. Actions are in motion, but then, unexpectedly, life throws you a curveball. Perhaps a friend with good intentions casts doubt on your goals, questioning their realism. Or, despite your diligent efforts, obstacles seem to mount—challenges, delays, and unforeseen circumstances, all seemingly conspiring against your aspirations.

This, my friend, is a natural and beautiful part of the journey. In fact, whether you realize it or not, these setbacks are designed to support your goal. Setbacks push us to grow, and growth is often a prerequisite to achieving our goals. It leads us to manifest the very experiences necessary for our evolution.

128

Consider Brian, a budding Tarot reader and intuitive healer. His path seemed clear—he had a vision to provide online Tarot readings and a plan to serve a specific audience. His initial steps were confident: building a website to kick-start his dream. But fate had other plans. His website developer disappeared midproject, and at launch, technical glitches with his payment system stalled client transactions. Month after month, Brian faced hurdle after hurdle.

In these moments of constant struggle, Brian paused to reflect. While his heart was set on online Tarot readings, the Universe seemed to be nudging him elsewhere. Attuning to this message, he shifted his focus, pivoting toward intuitive coaching within his local community. This realignment brought a swift change—clients flowed in, his reputation grew, and soon, a waiting list emerged for his services.

Brian's experience illustrates a profound truth in the art of manifesting: sometimes the Universe's plan diverges from our own. These experiences are meant to realign and elevate us to a vibrational frequency that resonates with our true goals—so we may fully participate in cocreating the best possible outcome with the Universe. These trials, if we embrace them, can transform us into a vibrational match for our desires. If we resist, they manifest as recurrent blocks as we continue to navigate a path not in alignment with our Higher Self. Trust that you are manifesting the very experiences necessary for your evolution and to bring you onto your ideal way forward.

Remember: each obstacle is a part of your journey. Trust in the Universe's grand plan, knowing that everything is unfolding in perfect harmony for your Highest Good. Stay positive, keep advancing, and remain devoted to your goals. Patience and trust are your allies in this adventure, opening your heart to a wealth of possibilities and letting the Universe surprise and delight you in its own perfect timing.

SURRENDER AND EMBRACE DIVINE TIMING

In our quest to manifest our dreams, we often forget a crucial player: the Universe's time line. My own journey has taught me that despite our best efforts, things unfold in their unique, often mysterious timing, which may not always match our personal schedules. This is where trust and surrender come into play. It's about believing that the Universe is supporting your Highest Good, even when it seems out of sync with your plans.

Consider Sophia's experience: after years of visualizing her dream home, it was her embrace of detachment and surrender to divine timing that brought her desires into reality in mere months.

Or look at Elena's story: aiming to find a new apartment in a weekend, she set a clear vision and took direct actions without overly attaching to any specific outcome. It was her trust and surrender that led her to secure her ideal home swiftly.

If we can release our tight grip on timing and specific outcomes and instead tune in to the essence of our desires, we will allow the Universe to work its magic. And it will often conjure up even more wondrous opportunities than we initially envisioned.

THE STAR:
ILLUMINATING YOUR PATH

The Star card of Tarot gleams as a beacon of hope, renewal, and freedom from the shackles of limiting beliefs. Rich in profound symbolism, the Star serves as a celestial guide through the journey of uncovering blocks, navigating doubts, and mastering the art of trust and surrender.

The Star card depicts a naked woman—a symbol of vulnerability and authenticity—gracefully positioned at the edge of a serene pool. This imagery speaks to us about shedding fears and doubts to reveal our truest selves. Her act of pouring water signifies the continuous flow of life and the nurturing of our spiritual paths, echoing themes of rejuvenation and growth.

Her balanced stance, with one foot on land and the other in water, represents the harmonious blend of practical wisdom and intuition. This equilibrium is essential in releasing limiting beliefs, as we align our conscious efforts with the profound wisdom of our subconscious.

The celestial backdrop of the Star, adorned with a radiant large star with seven smaller ones in the woman's hair, symbolizes our connection to the Divine and the alignment of our chakras. This starry scene inspires us with the limitless possibilities and immense potential within. This is especially true after periods of upheaval, as the Star follows the Tower in the Tarot sequence.

Manifesting with the Star's Energy

Invoking the Star's energy in our manifesting practice opens us to a world of hope and faith. It's a time to embrace the Universe's blessings and embark on a journey filled with peace, love, and profound personal growth.

Embracing Renewal and Hope: The Star encourages us to hold fast to hope and trust in the Universe's benevolence. This phase is about daring to dream big as we recognize that our aspirations are within reach.

Balancing Intuition and Practicality: Reflecting the woman in the card, we are urged to find a balance between our practical abilities and intuition. This balance is key in overcoming limiting beliefs, grounding our dreams in reality as we stay attuned to our inner guidance.

Connecting with Our Core Essence: The Star invites us to shed any facades and live authentically. This phase is about rediscovering or reaffirming our sense of purpose, inspiration, and meaning.

Cultivating a Generous Spirit: The energy of the Star extends beyond personal growth, inspiring us to share our blessings. It nurtures a spirit of generosity, reminding us that in giving, we receive and grow.

Listening to the Still Voice Within: The Star beckons us to listen to our inner wisdom and to be open to new ideas and paths. It's about trusting that inner voice and letting it guide us toward our highest potential.

— ◌◐◑◌ —

The Star in Tarot is a powerful symbol of hope, renewal, and spiritual enlightenment. Its energy supports us in breaking free from limiting beliefs, guiding us to trust in the Universe, embrace our authentic selves, and remain open to the boundless possibilities that await. As we align with the energy of the Star, we light up the path to manifesting our deepest desires and dreams, buoyed by its radiant guidance and wisdom.

INTUITIVE MANIFESTATION IN PRACTICE: TRUST THE PROCESS

When you encounter setbacks, limitations, fear, and doubt along the way, know that it is all happening for a reason. The Universe is simply offering you information about what is and isn't in alignment with your goals.

How you respond is paramount. You can choose to ignore the signs—but trust me, they will only continue to get louder until you pay attention. Or you can meet them head-on, knowing that they are here to serve you. Whether it's pesky procrastination, limiting beliefs, or impatience, there's a gift in each one.

What it ultimately boils down to is—trust the process. Trust that everything is happening for you, not against you. Look for the gifts. Seek out the subtle signs and information. And let these guide you toward what you truly desire—even if that means making some hard decisions along the way.

Of course, Tarot can support you in this process. When you feel your trust in the Universe wavering, use this spread:

1. **What is the deeper significance of this setback?**

2. **What lessons does this challenge reveal about my path to manifestation?**

3. **How can I realign my energy to resonate with my true desires?**

4. **What new actions are necessary for me to take now?**

5. **What outcomes might unfold if I embrace these new directions?**

Create a tranquil space. Draw a card for each question. And immerse yourself in their insights. I hope it helps you find a sense of peace and trust within.

MOVING FORWARD

Congratulations on reaching this pivotal point in your intuitive manifesting journey. As you move forward, remember the power lies in the practice. Keep revisiting these techniques whenever you encounter blocks or challenges. Each technique is not just a method, but a stepping stone toward deeper understanding and greater alignment with your goals. Remember: every step, no matter how small, is leading toward realizing your dreams. Your journey is unique, and each challenge is an opportunity to apply your newfound wisdom, refine your approach, and strengthen your resolve.

Trust is your compass on this journey. Put faith in your path, in the wisdom you've gained, and in the Universe's mysterious yet benevolent ways. Each manifestation, big or small, is a testament to your power and a celebration of your journey. With every success, your confidence will soar, and your ability to manifest will grow stronger.

But this is just the beginning. The path ahead is shimmering with even more potential and magic ready to be unlocked in the next chapter.

CHAPTER SEVEN:

Supercharge Your Results

PICTURE YOURSELF IN THE MIDST OF YOUR MANIFESTING: vision set, goals outlined, energy aligned, actions in motion. But then there comes a twist—the initial spark dims, your focus blurs, and your motivation dwindles as the early excitement dissolves into routine. This was a reality Sabina faced on her path to body alignment, as she strove for a healthier lifestyle filled with nutritious eating and daily, joyful movement.

Sabina's early efforts started with a bang; each day brought homemade, nutrient-packed meals and revitalizing walks. Slowly, her body began to transform. However, the scales told a different story. Despite her diligent efforts, the weight loss was gradual and not as rapid as Sabina had hoped. She couldn't yet fit into her most cherished dress, which was still hanging in her closet in anticipation. Disappointment and disenchantment crept in, overshadowing the progress she had made.

Sabina vented her frustration during a heart-to-heart with a dear friend, who was quick to point out the transformation Sabina was overlooking. "You radiate vibrancy, your skin glows, and there's a newfound joy in you," her friend reflected. That moment was a revelation. Yes, Sabina had indeed manifested remarkable changes. She might not have reached her desired weight, but she had fostered significant, positive transformations in her life.

From then on, Sabina shifted her focus to these "mini manifestations"—the tangible progress, the subtle shifts. Gratitude for her rejuvenated outlook on life, the slightly looser fit of her jeans, and the surge in her energy levels became Sabina's new focus. This change in perspective reignited her passion and commitment.

This is where you step in. I want you to envision not just achieving your dreams, but doing so with unprecedented ease and alignment. Whether it's feeling comfortable in your body, landing your dream job, or any other aspiration, embrace this phase with the full force of your intuitive power and the Universe's magic. This is your moment to shine as a masterful manifestor, channeling the Universe's energy and your own intuition to realize your goals in harmony and balance.

THE TRANSFORMATIVE POWER OF GRATITUDE AND CELEBRATION

If you want to supercharge your manifestations, the secret lies in focusing your energy and attention on the abundance that surrounds you. Remember our deep dive into the Universal Laws of Manifesting? The Law of Attraction was clear: what you focus on grows. So when your gaze lingers on the negatives, that's what proliferates in your life. Shift your focus to the positives and watch them flourish—that's the path we aspire to tread!

This is why gratitude and celebration aren't just nice thoughts; they're the engines driving your manifestation efforts. By celebrating your wins and expressing gratitude, you're essentially laying out a welcome mat for more abundance and success to enter your life.

Now, I know the idea of a daily gratitude practice might sound worn out. But bear with me, because gratitude is an astounding amplifying force when it comes to manifesting your goals.

Here's what your daily gratitude practice might look like. Each day, jot down five things you're grateful for. As you write these down, really sense the feeling of gratitude in every cell of your body, and then send that gratitude out into the world to reach those who need it most. Try this for just one week. The transformation in your mindset and your manifestation journey might just take you by surprise.

To supercharge your manifesting results, make it a habit to celebrate your daily wins, big or small. There's no need to wait for the ultimate goal to be achieved. By acknowledging and celebrating each step that brings you closer to your goal, you affirm your progress and stay aligned with your successful trajectory. It doesn't have to be groundbreaking. Maybe it's that extra mile you walked, a compliment from a friend, or a surprise find of a coin on the street. Recognizing these small wins creates the environment for your dreams to flourish and embeds the feelings of success deep within your journey.

Then, when you reach a significant milestone, make sure you pull out all the stops! Whether it's a serene day off, a luxurious treatment at your local spa, or a feast at your favorite restaurant, choose what fills your heart with joy and gratitude. And even better, plan these celebrations ahead of time—consider your next big milestone and make a commitment to how you will mark that victory.

You can, of course, consult Tarot cards to help you tap into the fulfilling energy of gratitude and celebration. Use the following spread either as part of your daily gratitude and celebration practice or simply when you need a little more intuitive insight.

The Gratitude Card: This card shines a light on an element of your journey that deserves gratitude. Ponder its message, and express thanks for the specific energy it radiates.

The Progress Card: Symbolizing your journey's advancements, this card invites you to celebrate your growth and the path you've traversed.

The Guidance Card: Offering direction for your ongoing manifestation, this card is your beacon for further progress and celebration.

Put down your thoughts and revelations from these cards in your journal. The insights you'll uncover can be eye-opening.

Embracing gratitude and celebration transforms your manifesting journey, making each step a powerful affirmation of your progress. These practices do more than acknowledge the good; they attract abundance and success. By infusing your daily life with gratitude and recognizing every win, you align with the Universe's abundant energy. Let Tarot be your guide as you turn gratitude into a magnetic force for your deepest desires.

As we move deeper into the final phase of the Intuitive Manifesting Method, it's time to enrich your tool kit with an essential element: positive affirmations. These affirmations play a pivotal role in shaping your mindset and influencing your actions, bringing you ever closer to achieving your goals.

HARNESSING THE POWER
OF POSITIVE AFFIRMATIONS
IN MANIFESTATION

Positive affirmations are far more than just uplifting sayings—they are dynamic instruments of change. When you regularly affirm your strengths, abilities, and potential, you set in motion a series of transformative processes:

Attracting Positive Energy: In harmony with the Law of Attraction, these affirmations foster a positive vibrational state. This positive vibration becomes a magnet, drawing in the people, resources, and opportunities crucial for achieving your goals.

Reprogramming the Subconscious: As highlighted in step 3 of the Intuitive Manifesting Method, your subconscious mind—the driver of your habits, actions, and decisions—gets reshaped. It begins to replace limiting beliefs with empowering ones, subtly steering your life toward positivity.

Building Self-Confidence: By constantly affirming your capabilities, you solidify your self-belief and your power to reach your goals. This surge in confidence equips you to tackle challenges, push through setbacks, and maintain your drive.

— ⊙◖◗⊙ —

While affirmations are a well-known tool in personal development, their impact is profound and far-reaching. To truly manifest your desires, a positive, empowering mindset is essential—and affirmations are potent in building this outlook.

Affirmations can be personalized to enhance your manifestation efforts. You can opt for universal affirmations or ones specifically aligned with your goals.

Here are some universal manifesting affirmations:

"What I desire flows to me with ease and grace."

"I am a beacon for my dreams and aspirations."

"Every step I take serves my Highest Good."

"Success is unfolding in my life right now."

"I embrace and accept myself unconditionally."

For targeted goals, like financial success, consider affirmations like:

"I attract financial opportunities and prosperity effortlessly."

"I am worthy of financial abundance; wealth flows to me naturally."

"Money finds its way to me, from both expected and unexpected sources."

"I am thankful for the continuous financial blessings in my life."

Crafting positive affirmations involves choosing statements that resonate with your aspirations and counteract limiting beliefs. For instance, if you want to attract wealth, affirmations like "I am capable of attracting financial abundance" are on target. Choose

143

affirmations that feel genuine and empowering; they should resonate with your beliefs and ignite enthusiasm within you.

Your Tarot cards can guide you in selecting affirmations. Simply pull a card, asking for some inspiration on where to focus, and let the card speak to you. Drawing a card like the Two of Swords could suggest an affirmation such as, "I make decisions with ease and confidence," which will help clarify and strengthen your decision-making.

The key to harnessing the power of affirmations is consistency. Make it a daily practice to vocalize your affirmations—perhaps several times a day. Place them on cards or sticky notes as visual reminders. Each repetition embeds these positive beliefs deeper into your psyche.

Positive affirmations transcend mere trends—they are timeless pillars of personal empowerment. When chosen thoughtfully and expressed with genuine emotion and conviction, they create a cascade of positive energy, attracting more positivity into your life while simultaneously dispelling negativity. The more you affirm, the more your self-assurance flourishes, propelling you forward in your journey of manifestation.

Remember, your connection with the Universe is a dynamic exchange of intuitive insights. Every step you take, every result—whether favorable or otherwise—offers valuable guidance. Stay aligned with your goals, adapt as necessary, and understand that there is no good or bad—every experience is a signpost pointing you toward or away from your true path.

EXPERIENCE THE MAGIC
(AND EXPECT MORE!)

Having established a solid foundation through gratitude, celebration, and positive affirmations in manifesting your goals, it's time to embrace a phase of ease and openness. While aligned action is vital in intuitive manifesting, it's equally important to avoid overextending yourself. This is the moment to transition into a state of receptivity, allowing the Universe's magic to unfold naturally.

Consider Elena's experience: she set a clear intention to find a new apartment in one weekend. After initiating action by contacting agents, she shifted into a mode of surrender, trusting the Universe to deliver. Her relaxed approach led to a successful outcome by the weekend's end.

In this state of receptivity, you'll begin to notice blessings, surprises, and small victories that confirm your path. These experiences channel your energy toward your desires, fostering their growth (echoing the Law of Attraction and Law of Vibration).

You'll also find intuitive nudges guiding you—some affirming your course, others signaling the need for adjustment. It's like fine-tuning the sails on a yacht to ensure a smooth, efficient journey to your goal.

Integrate Tarot into this practice by regularly seeking its guidance. Ask questions like, "How am I in alignment with my goal? What adjustments are needed?" Record these insights and observe the shifts over time.

Additionally, stay attuned to the signals life presents—be they green lights of encouragement or red flags calling for a course correction.

Remember: pausing for quiet reflection is essential in manifesting. It's about tuning in, listening to the wisdom within, and adapting as needed. This journey is not just about action; it's about aligning with your highest frequency, letting the magic of the Universe flow through you, and welcoming the abundance that's yet to come.

BEYOND ACHIEVEMENT TO TRANSFORMATION

Often, the true triumph in this process lies not only in achieving specific milestones, but also in the enduring transformations sparked by intuitive manifesting. These deep shifts extend beyond immediate goals, laying the foundation for more substantial and expansive changes in our lives.

Consider Anne's journey, for example. Her aim was to deepen her connections and enrich her relationships with her friends. The journey toward building substantial friendships was gradual, yet all along the way Anne witnessed a remarkable transformation in her own behavior—more initiative in forming bonds and breaking past barriers. As she progressed, Anne realized her lifestyle needed a tweak—more self-care, healthier eating, adequate sleep, and space for these budding friendships. Here, the magic unfolds: her new goals aren't a diversion but a natural progression and an evolution of her initial aspiration. This pattern isn't exclusive to personal connections. It applies universally—in professional endeavors, relationship dynamics, or enhancing your personal space. Anne's story beautifully encapsulates the essence of intuitive manifesting—it's a journey of setting intentions, adapting, overcoming obstacles, and embracing the transformational path.

Then there's Alicia, who sought a deeper connection with her husband of three decades. Her tool? Tarot. Incorporating Tarot into her manifesting practice piqued her husband's interest, and this evolved into daily readings. But the real prize was the deeper conversations that emerged between the two during these sessions, as they engaged in discussions about their hopes, their dreams, and the future. This shared interest in Tarot morphed their relationship from distant coexistence to a rekindled romantic connection.

Anne and Alicia's experiences show how your manifestation journey can grow and adapt as you embrace new aspirations along the way. As you advance, your initial goals may evolve, leading to new insights and desires. Welcome this change. Revisit your goals with these fresh perspectives, weaving them into your ongoing journey while they enrich rather than replace your original ambitions. This cyclical process of goal setting, achieving, and resetting is an integral, dynamic aspect of manifestation.

As you venture forward, remember that manifestation is an ongoing cycle. Each achieved goal, each gained insight, is a doorway to fresh possibilities. Be it in career growth, relationship enrichment, or personal well-being, each move forward draws you nearer to a life that's more aligned and fulfilling. The key is to stay receptive to this ever-evolving journey, savoring each achievement and seamlessly integrating new aspirations as they emerge.

Utilizing the Law of Attraction isn't just about magnifying your success; it's about creating a vibrant, visual chronicle of your growth. Every small step is a leap forward, propelling you closer to realizing your dreams each day. Soon, you'll discover you are closer to actualizing your dreams than you ever imagined was possible.

THE SUN

THE SUN: SHINE BRIGHT!

Our Tarot Guide for this step is the Sun. The Sun is a beacon of celebration, gratitude, and the amplification of your creative essence. It's a vibrant symbol of life's triumphs and the generous support of the Universe, vividly captured in its radiant imagery.

A wellspring of positivity and vitality, this card showcases a resplendent Sun, which is not just a source of physical wellness but also a beacon guiding us to success and abundance.

Beneath this life-affirming Sun, four robust sunflowers stand tall, echoing the four suits of the Minor Arcana and the elements. These flowers are emblems of growth, stability, and balanced energy, reminding us that our dreams and goals are nurtured by the harmonious blend of life's diverse aspects.

At the heart of the card, a child exudes pure joy, symbolizing an intimate connection with our inner spirit and the unfiltered happiness of childhood. The child's nakedness signifies transparency and authenticity—a celebration of our truest selves. The white horse, a sign of purity and strength, carries the child forward on a journey of clarity and purpose.

Manifesting with the Sun's Radiance

When we invoke the Sun's energy in our manifestation practices, we open ourselves to a world of celebration, gratitude, and uplifting vibrations.

Embracing the Spirit of Celebration and Gratitude: The Sun invites us to revel in our accomplishments and appreciate life's gifts. This cycle of celebration and thankfulness sets the stage for attracting further abundance and achievements.

Cultivating Positivity: The Sun encourages us to maintain an optimistic mindset, thereby drawing favorable experiences and connections into our orbit.

Fostering Inner Joy and Authenticity: Echoing the child on the card, the Sun urges us to reconnect with our inner joy and authentic self. This bond enhances playfulness and genuineness, which are essential for a fulfilling journey of manifestation.

Drawing Strength from Life's Challenges: The message of the Sun is uplifting—it teaches us that through challenges we find growth and meaning. It reassures us of the brighter times ahead and the attainability of success.

Harnessing Your Inner Power: The Sun connects us with our core strength, which emanates from the solar plexus chakra. It encourages us to use our divine will and inner fortitude to express ourselves authentically and make a meaningful impact.

Experiencing Renewed Vitality and Enthusiasm: Symbolizing energy and zest, the Sun heralds a period of heightened physical and emotional vigor, revitalizing us and fueling our passion for life.

— ⟡ —

The Sun is a powerful emblem of achievement, radiance, and prosperity. Its energy empowers us in our quest to enhance our results, prompting us to embrace gratitude, celebrate our victories, and recognize the Universe's unwavering support. As we align with the Sun's energy, our manifestations are magnified, and we bask in the glow of our successes and the endless opportunities that lie ahead.

INTUITIVE MANIFESTING IN PRACTICE: EMBRACING JOY AND TRANSFORMATION

When it comes to intuitive manifesting, celebration and gratitude walk hand in hand. The Universe thrives on joy, and your manifesting journey should be a delightful adventure. Celebrate every milestone, regardless of its size! You can mark the occasion with something as simple or as lavish as you like—from savoring a piece of chocolate to enjoying a bubble bath, nurturing a new plant, or even having an impromptu dance party in your kitchen. The important thing is to consciously acknowledge and revel in each success.

Make it a daily practice to visualize your goals and desires as already realized. Step into the energy of the person you are becoming to achieve these dreams. *Be Then Do.* Rejoice in the progress you've made and feel a deep sense of gratitude for your accomplishments, as well as a thrilling anticipation for what is still to unfold.

Next, focus on your immediate aligned action. Ask yourself: *What one step can I take today or this week to edge closer to my goals?* Be aware of any obstacles or self-doubt that emerge and address them using the strategies we've discussed.

Incorporate your positive affirmations regularly to experience magic, relax into receiving, and listen carefully to the nudges from the Universe as you stay aligned with your path.

As you integrate this ritual into your daily life, you'll notice a transformative shift. What starts as a structured task evolves into a genuine desire and, eventually, becomes an innate aspect of your being. You'll find yourself effortlessly envisioning your future, embodying the necessary characteristics for success, taking steps in alignment with your aspirations, overcoming hurdles, and magnifying your achievements.

This practice is not just a series of actions; it's a metamorphosis of your entire approach to life and goals. Through Tarot, you are not just visualizing and striving for specific outcomes, but instead aligning with a deeper, more authentic part of yourself. You're learning to live in harmony with your highest potential, tuning in to your inner guidance, and embracing the journey as much as the destination.

As you continue to practice intuitive manifesting with Tarot, it becomes more than a ritual; it becomes a way of life. A life where every day is an opportunity to manifest, to grow, and to celebrate the magic that surrounds you. Embrace this journey with an open heart, and let Tarot guide you toward a life filled with more joy, fulfillment, and success.

EMPOWERED MANIFESTATION: YOUR COMPLETE TOOL KIT FOR SUCCESS

With the four steps of the Intuitive Manifesting Method now at your fingertips, you have access to an extensive array of resources to support your manifesting journey. This includes guided visualizations, insightful Tarot spreads, intuitive reflections, and a wealth of other tools designed to amplify your practice.

It's important to remember that the steps outlined in this method are not meant to be rigidly linear. Instead, trust your intuition to lead you to the right tool at the right time. These resources are now an integral part of your tool kit, always available to assist you whenever you feel the call.

And with that, you are fully equipped to excel as a manifesting maestro. Have faith in the process and engage wholeheartedly with the journey. As you do, you'll witness the remarkable unfolding of your dreams and goals as they materialize into your reality.

Embrace this path with confidence and enthusiasm. The tools and knowledge you've acquired are not just techniques; they're catalysts for transformation and growth. They empower you to connect deeply with your desires, align your actions with your highest purpose, and create a life that resonates with your truest self.

So step forward boldly. You're not just practicing a method; you're embarking on a profound adventure of self-discovery and manifestation. Trust in yourself, in the power of the Universe, and in the journey you are on. Watch in awe as the world responds to your intentions and your dreams begin to take shape right before your eyes.

Remember: in the world of intuitive manifesting, you are both the creator and the creation, the dreamer and the dream. Embrace this journey with all its twists and turns, for it is in this journey that the true magic lies.

˳ ° ○ ✳ ○ ° ˳

CHAPTER EIGHT:

Becoming a
Manifestation Magnet

IN THIS CONCLUDING CHAPTER, LET'S REVISIT THE HEART
of the Intuitive Manifesting Method and place everything you've
learned into a broader perspective. My intention here is clear:
I want to help you internalize this method so deeply that mani-
festing becomes not just a series of actions but a state of being. We
know that the most incredible results stem from *being* then *doing*

rather than the reverse. My hope is that you'll embody intuitive manifesting, allowing your powerful, creative energy to flow naturally and effortlessly whenever you set a goal.

And just look at how far you've already come! You tapped into your deepest mental reserves and unlocked your manifesting potential.

You Envisioned Your Perfect Future. You moved beyond the surface of your desires through self-reflection, visualization, and journaling. You set your intentions, aligning them with your Highest Good, guided by the wisdom of Tarot.

You Became an Energetic Match for Your Desires. You learned to step into a future version of yourself, embodying the necessary traits to attract your desired outcome. You took aligned action, embracing the philosophy of *Be Then Do*.

You Overcame Blocks and Limiting Beliefs. You explored and addressed common manifestation blocks, and, understanding that blockages can arise at any time, you equipped yourself with strategies to tackle them, transforming obstacles into stepping stones.

You Amplified Your Success. You've embraced gratitude and celebrated each of your successes. And you are in a place of serene receptivity, where you can effortlessly flow with the tides of life, making adjustments with grace and ease as the winds of gratitude fill your sails.

— ◦⬦◦ —

The journey doesn't end here. You're now armed with powerful steps and an abundance of intuitive strategies, Tarot techniques, and visualizations to empower you wherever your path leads.

I trust that you now recognize your Tarot cards are invaluable guides, mentors, and advisors, intricately connecting you with your intuition and inner wisdom. The spreads you've engaged with are enduring treasures, offering insights and guidance you can revisit time and again.

You are now fully equipped to manifest your desires, whether they're related to wealth, love, freedom, connection, or any other aspect of life. Your potential is limitless, and you are poised for incredible success. Should doubts arise—and it's natural that they might—trust that you have the mindset and the necessary tools to navigate through them.

Reflect on your progress by revisiting your journal entries. Celebrate your evolution and progress as an intuitive manifestor and creator of your reality. Acknowledge your achievements, whether you've reached your original goal or are well on your way.

And as you reach your big milestones and achieve your goals, I would love to hear how you're applying the Intuitive Manifesting Method. Reach out to me via Instagram (@biddytarot) or email (team@biddytarot.com) so we can celebrate your success alongside you.

Celebration is not just encouraged—it's essential! In your journal, note at least five of your biggest wins since starting this program. Yes! Right now! How have you transformed? What strides have you made toward your goals? Share your victories and celebrate them in a way that fills your soul with joy.

Embrace your newfound identity as a vibrant and effective manifestor. Remember, if you can visualize it and align with it, you can achieve it. The path ahead is bright, and there truly are no limits to what you can accomplish—and the more you do, the more effortless it becomes.

MAKE MANIFESTATION A LIFESTYLE

While it's outlined as a linear process in these pages, the Intuitive Manifesting Method truly unfolds in a dynamic, nonlinear fashion. Instead of walking a straight line, it's more like climbing a mountain. At first, you might meticulously follow each step—with cautious walking, regular hydration, vigilant path observation, and navigating obstacles, much like a beginner climber.

As you ascend, pausing periodically to savor the stunning views, you realize your route spirals upward around the mountain. Each loop, combining careful movement, hydration, observation, rest, and admiration, might feel repetitive, but it incrementally elevates you, drawing you closer to the summit.

Gradually, as you become more adept and confident in your journey, these actions start to seamlessly merge and occur in unison. Practices that once demanded conscious effort now flow effortlessly.

This is the essence of intuitive manifesting. You begin by concentrating on individual steps—setting intentions, taking aligned actions, overcoming obstacles, and embracing amplification. Over time, as these practices become woven into the fabric of your daily life, they naturally integrate and intersect, evolving from distinct actions into a harmonious, instinctive process. You might find yourself clearing blocks while envisioning the future or practicing gratitude while taking aligned action.

The biggest revelation of this program is that it's not just about following a four-step process and then being done. It's about adopting a new way of living, a daily approach to realizing your dreams and becoming the creator of your own life.

This is the essence of living a manifesting lifestyle in which every day becomes an act of creation, of shaping your destiny. This is not a method to be followed and then set aside; it's a lifelong way of being.

And this is why integrating Tarot with manifestation techniques is so transformative. Tarot itself is a powerful tool for self-creation. I'm sure you've already seen how potent this synergy can be.

The Intuitive Manifesting Method, coupled with the intuitive power of Tarot, unlocks a remarkable capability within you. As Ann shares, "Integrating Intuitive Manifesting into my daily life and my burgeoning Tarot and coaching business has been transformative. It's a powerful model that grounds me, keeping me focused on my goals. Sharing this with friends has been a joy, and I'm excited to extend it further."

BE A GUIDING LIGHT FOR OTHERS

Kristine was already a successful motivation and manifestation coach, but she felt called to expand her practice even further. When she discovered the power of intuitive manifesting and Tarot, it was a revelation. She began using Tarot to help her clients connect with their energy, identify their desires, and align with their Highest Good. Initially hesitant about how her clients might perceive her use of Tarot, she soon found them enthralled by the insights, which significantly enhanced their manifesting journeys. This unique approach not only led her clients to remarkable achievements and transformations but also set Kristine apart from other coaches. Her practice flourished as a result. She attracted more clients and witnessed their continuous growth (and saw them return for further guidance).

When you begin to see the fruits of your manifesting, others will take notice too. You might hear comments like, "You seem different," or "You're achieving so much lately!" You might even be asked, "Please tell me your secret!" This is your opportunity to share your story, not just as a celebration of your achievements, but as a beacon of inspiration, showing others that they, too, can tap into this powerful creative process.

However, there are times when your transformations may unsettle those around you, leading to skepticism or misunderstanding from friends or family. Understand that this doesn't mean you're off course. Instead, it's often a sign that you're realigning your life, shedding what no longer serves your purpose—much like the Tower card in Tarot, which precedes profound transformation. After this phase of disruption (or even upheaval) comes the Star—a time of renewal, clarity, and truth.

As you reflect on the positive shifts in your life, consider how you might radiate these changes outward. Equipped with these manifestation tools, you might feel called to guide others, perhaps as a Tarot reader, coach, healer, or empowerment practitioner. Incorporating these techniques into your professional practice can profoundly impact others, contributing to the collective lifting in global consciousness and vibrational energy.

Alternatively, you may choose to keep these practices personal to you, which is equally valid.

If you're drawn to expand your influence and assist others, ponder these questions:

- **How can I leverage this new approach to manifesting to benefit my friends and family?**

- **How can I positively influence others now that I understand my role as the creator of my destiny?**

- **What is my Higher Purpose in relation to manifestation?**

Consider journaling your thoughts on these questions, then consulting Tarot for further insights, recording any revelations for future reflection.

As Paulo Coelho aptly states, "Happiness is contagious." Your transformation will naturally attract others, and you may feel compelled to share your journey. Embrace this opportunity. By spreading positivity and empowerment, you contribute to a ripple effect of change and growth.

THE WORLD: MANIFESTATION, COMPLETION, AND RENEWAL

The World Tarot card stands majestically as a beacon of completion, integration, and the dawn of new cycles, encapsulating the essence of becoming a potent manifestor and a guiding light for others. This card represents the culmination of the transformative journey you've embarked upon, through which you've become equipped with newfound wisdom and tools.

The World stands as a majestic symbol of the culmination of your transformative journey as a potent manifestor and guiding light for others. It represents not just completion and integration, but also the dawn of new cycles—marking a significant milestone in your path of personal and spiritual growth.

Just look at how deeply symbolic the World's imagery is: The laurel wreath speaks to victory and eternal cycles, its circular shape representing the continuity of success and the seamless transition into new beginnings. The woman stepping through the wreath signifies the end of one journey and the immediate progression to the next, in a cycle of endless growth and rejuvenation.

Ah, and the fact that the woman is dancing!! Her dance is a celebration of freedom and achievement, illustrating the elation that accompanies the completion of a cycle. Her nudity stands for authenticity and vulnerability, for embracing one's true essence unreservedly.

The wands in her hands mirror those of the Magician, indicating that the journey of manifestation initiated by the Magician reaches its zenith with the World.

Finally, the four figures encircling the wreath symbolize the fixed zodiac signs and the four elements, which guide the seamless transition from one phase to another, ensuring balance and harmony.

Manifesting with the World's Energy

Let the World's energy infuse your manifesting practice when . . .

Celebrating Transitions: The World card encourages the celebration of achievements and the welcoming of new phases. It reminds us that endings are also beginnings and beckons us to move forward with joy and anticipation.

Integrating Wisdom: This card invites introspection and integration of the journey's lessons. Understanding how each experience has contributed to growth primes us for future manifestations.

Becoming a Beacon for Others: Embodying the World's energy transforms us into inspirations for others as we demonstrate the power and beauty of embracing life's cycles with gratitude and wisdom.

Moving Forward with Assurance: The World signals a time to confidently apply the knowledge and tools you've acquired, enhancing your manifesting skills and approaching new aspirations with a sense of completeness.

Expanding Perspectives: This card also encourages a broadened understanding, inviting us to view our journey within a global context and fostering a connection with the wider world.

— ◌◦◌ —

The World in Tarot symbolizes the full circle of life's journeys, representing fulfillment, unity, and ongoing evolution. Its energy fortifies us as manifesting magnets, guiding us to celebrate our entirety, welcome new chapters with assurance, and continue our journey with the enriched insight and creative energy we have nurtured. As we align with the World's energy, we are poised to embark on new paths and inspire others with our transformative journey, becoming guiding lights in the world of manifestation.

As you pause to reflect on the incredible journey you've embarked upon, it's essential to recognize the remarkable progress you've made since beginning this program. Think back to when you first started—the aspirations you held, the lessons you've learned, and the transformation you've undergone. This journey is a testament to your dedication and the power of intuitive manifesting.

You've gained invaluable tools and insights:

- **The Four-Step Intuitive Manifesting Method is now a part of your tool kit.**

- **Tarot has become your guide, aiding you in embodying the qualities necessary to achieve your goals.**

- **You've learned to align your aspirations with your highest potential and take actions that resonate with this alignment.**

- **Strategies for overcoming obstacles and releasing limiting beliefs are now at your fingertips.**

- **You've cultivated a practice of gratitude, affirmations, and celebrating successes.**

- **Guided visualizations and meditations have deepened your connection with your intuition and Higher Self.**

- **Tarot cards, along with various Tarot spreads, have illuminated your path toward your dreams.**

Remember: these tools are always available for you to draw on as you continue to manifest your dreams into reality. And as you progress, you'll discover even more resources to aid your journey.

Envision this next chapter of your life filled with confidence, courage, and success. Visualize everything falling into place, perfectly timed, with the Universe working in your favor.

Tarot, as you've likely discovered, is such a remarkable resource for growth in every area of your life. It's like having an ever-present mentor, guide, and teacher. Tarot's advice and insights continuously astound me with their depth and relevance. Should you feel the call to explore deeper into the world of Tarot and its potential to enrich your life, Biddy Tarot offers a wealth of resources. Whether you're curious about deepening your Tarot knowledge, expanding your reading skills to assist others, or even incorporating Tarot into your business, we have courses tailored to all these aspirations.

For those inspired by this program and considering starting or expanding a business, I'm particularly excited for you! Supporting healers, coaches, Tarot readers, and creatives in making a positive impact while growing their income is a passion of mine. Our unique business program is designed specifically for intuitive entrepreneurs like you.

Explore these opportunities at www.biddytarot.com/shop, and if you have questions about which path to choose, feel free to reach out to our team of success advisors at team@biddytarot .com. They're eager to provide personalized guidance for your next steps. And remember to access your free resources that go along with this book at www.biddytarot.com/imbook.

As we conclude, I have a request. If the Intuitive Manifesting Method has positively impacted your life, we'd love to hear your success story. Your experiences and feedback are invaluable—they inspire and inform our work. Please share your stories with us at team@biddytarot.com.

Thank you for your energy and trust, and for allowing Tarot to be a part of your journey. I eagerly anticipate continuing this journey with you and am honored to have been a stop on your path thus far.

· ∘ ○ ✳ ○ ∘ ·

ACKNOWLEDGMENTS & GRATITUDE

This book in itself has been a journey of intuitive manifesting—one filled with brilliant visions, aligned action, joyful surprises, and, of course, deep gratitude for the many people who have been a part of its creation. I wish to express my deep appreciation for . . .

Ann Maynard, my writing partner and editor, who made this book possible. When I started writing this book, I set a very clear intention that the creation process would unfold with ease and joy. Without Ann, I do not think this would have been possible! Ann masterfully breathed life and magic into my concepts, stories, and teachings, expressing the words beautifully in a way that felt true to my voice. I absolutely loved working with Ann, with her infectious enthusiasm and commitment to making words sparkle.

Fiona Lister, who worked with me on the original Intuitive Manifesting course that inspired this book. She turned my concepts and stories into vibrant video scripts for our online tutorials.

Shannon Fabricant and the Running Press team, for their collaborative spirit and unwavering enthusiasm to bring *Intuitive Manifesting* into the world.

Our Intuitive Manifesting course students, who courageously and generously shared their stories: the triumphs, the challenges, and everything in between. I am deeply grateful for the opportunity to watch their journeys and to walk alongside them as a coach and a guide.

Our entire Biddy Tarot community, who continue to transform their lives with Tarot. Seeing so many people activate their intuition with Tarot as a guide is such a joy. They inspire me every day to continue sharing this work with as many people as possible.

The Biddy Tarot team, who bring my vision to life so that we can impact millions. And a special shout-out to Kaileen Sherk for running the business and making sure I had the time, space, and energy to devote to this book.

My family—my husband, Anthony, and daughters, Chloe and Zara—for giving me the space to be who I am, to travel the world, to be inspired, to connect with people from all walks of life worldwide.

And, of course, you, my beloved Reader. Thank you for saying *yes* to *Intuitive Manifesting* and embracing the power and the magic of weaving your inner wisdom into your manifesting journey. May you be blessed with everything you have ever dreamed of and more!

INDEX